FALLEN OFFICERS OF THE WICHITA POLICE DEPARTMENT

1871-2024

Christopher P. Marceau

Published by Marceau Book Company LLC

Wichita, Kansas

Copyright © 2025 by Christopher P. Marceau

All rights reserved

Front cover: The Gold Wreath of Honor, the Wichita Police Department's highest award. November 15, 2024. Photo taken by Christopher P. Marceau.

Back cover: The top piece of the Sedgwick County Law Enforcement Memorial. November 23, 2024. Photo taken by Christopher P. Marceau.

First published 2025

Manufactured in the United States

Hardback ISBN 979-8-9924576-0-5

Paperback ISBN 979-8-9924576-1-2

Notice: The information in this book is true and complete to the best of the author's knowledge. It is offered without guarantee on the part of the author. The author disclaims all liability in connection with the use of this book.

All rights reserved. No portion of this book may be reproduced in any form without written permission from the publisher or author, except as permitted by U.S. copyright law.

For Amanda Lynn Marceau

Contents

Introduction	1
Wichita, Kansas	3
Part One	7
1. Patrolman John W. Kerwin	9
2. Patrolman Henry Ebenhack	13
3. Patrolman S. A. Hartzell	21
Part Two	27
4. Detective William L. Humphries	29
5. Captain Frank W. Griswold	34
6. Detective William H. Ballard	40
7. Patrolman Albert L. Young	49
8. Patrolman James R. Fitzpatrick	55
9. Detective Charles D. Hoffman	61
10. Detective Charles E. Galloway	66
11. Patrolman Robert C. Scudder	69
12. Patrolman Harrison R. Brown	76
13. Detective Edward W. Hall	81
14. Patrolman Vernon E. Ogden	91
15. Patrolman Joseph E. Marshall	95
16. Sergeant Paul E. Gilmore	103
17. Lieutenant James O. Pugh	107

18. Patrolman Merle R. Colver	110
Part Three	119
19. Patrolman David A. Kenyon	121
20. Officer Paul N. Garofalo	127
21. Officer Danny D. Laffey	136
22. Lieutenant John E. Galvin	140
23. Captain Clay M. Germany	143
Categorical Data and Historical Analysis	147
Case Analysis	161
Conclusion	167
Appendices	169
Appendix A	171
Appendix B	173
Appendix C	175
Bibliography	177
Acknowledgements	187
About the Author	189

INTRODUCTION

"Writing that contributes to the remembrance of others prevents them from dying a second time and allows our memories of them to live on."
- Christopher P. Marceau

Why would any person have a desire to learn the details of a tragic and depressing subject, such as law enforcement line of duty deaths?

The same question can be asked of history in general. It is full of catastrophic events that destroyed countless lives, whether from wars, crimes, or plagues. But the study of history has a purpose. You and I are not certain of what is going to happen in thirty seconds, thirty days, or thirty years from now, but we can predict it based on the history we know. And everything we know, at any moment in time, is history.

The truth is, the more knowledge we possess about the past, makes us better predictors of the future, and puts us in a better position to make wise decisions that will benefit us down the winding, rocky road (as no person's path is always straight, paved, and smooth).

Various benefits come with knowing history, to include a better understanding of people, cultures, and society, an enhanced contemplation of moral understanding, a feeling of identity as an individual, a family, a community, and a nation, useful applications in work environments, and even good citizenship.

That same concept also applies to those who work for police agencies everywhere, commissioned and non-commissioned alike. Police officers should have a strong interest in learning more about the sacrifices former officers made throughout the history of their department for several reasons: the research, study, and remembrance of events honors the officers that were killed in the line of duty.

Without knowledge, one cannot fully understand the culture; the same can be said for any organization, really.

The story of an officer's death can teach us something, especially young officers who do not have as much experience. The deaths of those men and women are not in vain, and we should not ignore their tales.

Officers who love history should find it humorous when a fellow co-worker in the department mentions their distaste for the subject, because their routine daily task of incident report generation, something no officer can fully escape, is an official contribution to the local history of the city or town they work in. Officers are constantly writing history, whether they know it or not, every time they pull a case number.

The following book is written by a police officer, with an intended audience largely consisting of police officers or those that are closely affiliated with them. The writing style is straight-forward and matter of fact, much like you see in a police report. It is not meant to embellish certain actions of those involved or give a false depiction of valor for every officer involved, but only to give a true account of how they died, an ethical obligation mandated of the author as an honest historian and police officer. And there are lessons to be learned in every incident in this book.

The City of Wichita, at the time of this writing, has been fortunate in recent years regarding line of duty deaths. The last murder of a Wichita police officer was Officer Paul Garofalo on November 8, 1980. When considering the size of Wichita, we realize how fortunate the city has been in recent years.

Three factors seem to be at play: luck, quick and effective medical attention, and good training. The implementation of better training and the FTO (Field Training Officer) program has provided safety benefits that we will never fully comprehend. Our goal should be a continuation of good and abundant training in the future, with the study of history included.

WICHITA, KANSAS

A Short History

Visualize life in the area known as Wichita, just after the Civil War; there were wide-open spaces with visibility for miles, some provisional-like structures that generally lacked architecture and style, and dusty trails leading to and from the place. Kansas, the thirty-fourth state admitted to the Union, was just an infant during the Civil War. While not called the Sunflower State in its early years, it was still seen by many people as a place that provided fresh starts and new opportunities.

In 1868, thirty people lived in the area where the Little Arkansas River and the Arkansas River joined together, with the number increasing to 689 just two years later. On July 21, 1870, with the stroke of Judge Reuben Riggs' pen, the articles of incorporation for Wichita, Kansas had been formally established. Wichita was officially a town.

Of the 689 people residing there, most residents were farmers. Others included housekeepers, a wagon maker, teamsters, photographers, a dentist, butchers, stonemasons, attorneys, blacksmiths, saddle and harness makers, cattle dealers, a stage driver, dry goods and grocery dealers, domestic servants, physicians, carpenters, schoolteachers, a house painter, a justice of the peace, real estate agents, clerks, a minister and, of course, saloon keepers. More than half of these people were unable to read and write. Housing at the time was problematic for some. Multiple generations often lived crowdedly under the same roof and some houses consisted of multiple families. While these times were tough for most folks in Wichita, the growing town established an entrepreneurial and innovative spirit that would last for decades.[1]

Wichita boomed in the 1870s with the murky cattle trade business, lasting about four years. Long drives of cattle, primarily from Texas, moved north on dusty trails, such

---

1. Beccy Tanner, *Bear Grease, Builders and Bandits: The Men and Women of Wichita's Past* (Wichita: The Wichita Eagle and Beacon Publishing Company, 1991), 10-11.

as the Chisolm Trail, to trains headed east. Businesspersons in Wichita, who generally were not cowboys themselves, made money by supplying commodities and vices for the worn-out cowboys.

In the early part of the twentieth century, Wichita saw substantial growth in the consumer goods industry. The place became a regional hub for wheat milling, meatpacking, stockyards, and broomcorn. Local businesses and the Wichita economy significantly expanded in the 1900s and 1910s. Investments in the oil industry in the 1910s led to the financing of aviation in Wichita, creating the pathway for the establishment of corporations like Beechcraft, Stearman, and Cessna.[2]

Being a police officer in the late 1910s was not an easy task. They worked the entire week with no days off, and their shift lasted twelve hours. An officer's pay in the mid-to-late teens was only ninety dollars a month, which calculates to $1,080 a year.[3] The relative value, using the Consumer Price Index, of $1,080 in 1917 is equal to $20,000 in 2015.[4]

Turnover of police officers and chiefs were high during this decade. In 1917, there were ninety officers in the Wichita Police Department. Samuel W. Zickefoose became chief of the Department in 1919 and oversaw policing Wichita's 83,702 inhabitants. However, in 1920, both the city's population and the number of police officers decreased. Sixty-one officers guarded a population of just over 72,000 people during this time.[5]

The 1910s were filled with new innovations and problems. The creation of the gasoline engine led to an abundance of vehicles and motorcycles on the streets of Wichita. Paved roads started to become a new norm, along with traffic and speeding problems. Drug addiction among people of all ages increased throughout the city, and so did criminal activity. Thefts, burglaries, and robberies alarmed both citizens and city officials, which led to the establishment of more city ordinances.[6] In this decade, it seemed like there was more of everything, good and bad.

---

2. Jay M. Price, *Wichita: 1860 – 1930* (Charleston: Arcadia Publishing, 2003), 7-8.

3. Jordan D. Jones, *The First Century: A History of the Wichita Police Department 1871 - 1979* (Wichita: Jostens, 1979), 29.

4. MeasuringWorth, accessed November 16, 2016, https://www.measuringworth.com/.

5. Jones, *First Century*, 29.

6. Roger E. Williamson, *Wichita Police Department: 1871-2000* (Wichita: Wichita Police Benefit Fund Association, 2001), 35-36.

Despite some ups and downs, the first fifty years generally were a growing and thriving period for Wichita. According to the United States Census Bureau, the population of Wichita in 1920 was 72,217.[7] While the City of Wichita today is over five times the size that it was in 1920, it was still on the list of the 100 largest cities in the United States. As the city grew, so did the size of the police force.

Unfortunately, as readers will see in later chapters, the 1910s, 1920s, and 1930s saw a dramatic increase of murder among those that protected Wichita and its residents, as opposed to the tragedies in 1888, where careless and negligent behavior took the lives of two out of three officers.

Tragic events like the ones discussed in this book often prompt dramatic changes in policy and procedures throughout police departments everywhere and often highlight the deficiencies of the department. The goal of this book is that the study of line of duty deaths will help prevent them, either by an increase in knowledge or sparking a need for change away from poor practices and policies.

---

7. "Population of the 100 Largest Urban Places: 1920," U.S. Census Bureau, accessed October 27, 2016, https://www.census.gov/population/www/documentation/twps0027/tab15.txt.

Part One

The Forgotten Three: Casualties of a Young, Booming City with Few Rules, Little Experience, and Unstable Leadership

1

Patrolman John W. Kerwin

Date: March 23, 1888
Day: Friday
Time: 1010 hours
Location: 903 East Douglas Avenue
Tour: Eight Weeks (1888)
Age: Forty-seven or forty-eight
Race: White
Gender: Male
Marital Status: Married
Military Veteran: Unknown
Children: Eight
Badge: Not applicable
Burial: Calvary Cemetery, Wichita, Sedgwick County, Kansas
Cause: Gunfire (accidental)
Weapon: .38 caliber revolver
Offender Status: Not applicable
Offender Age: Not applicable
Offender Race: Not applicable
Offender Gender: Not applicable
City Marshal at the Time: William W. Haines

Drawing of Patrolman John W. Kerwin accidentally shooting himself. The Wichita Daily Journal. March 23, 1888. Public Domain.

Patrolman John W. Kerwin was killed in an accidental shooting at 1010 hours on Friday, March 23, 1888, at 903 East Douglas Avenue.

The incident occurred inside a little second-hand store owned by William Christianson, a German man who immigrated to the United States and made his way to Wichita. Christianson and Kerwin were standing at the showcase counter discussing the trade of Kerwin's duty revolver for a different type that was on display, when Christianson asked the officer to see his weapon. Just before Kerwin handed over the gun to Christianson, it was discharged into Kerwin's chest, striking the heart. After being shot, Kerwin stated, "Oh, my God!" and dropped to the floor.[1]

A nickel-plated double action .38 caliber bulldog-patterned revolver was the deadly instrument that took the policeman's life and laid beside him when a reporter arrived on scene. Approximately 300 people crowded around the store twenty minutes after the incident, but they were unable to enter the locked doors after Chief Haines gave orders to

---

1. "Through the Heart," *The Wichita Beacon*, March 23, 1888.

allow only authorized people to enter. Dr. H. C. Hood indicated the death was immediate when the round traveled through the heart.

Kerwin was survived by his wife and eight children. "Quiet Kerwin," as he was called, worked for the Department for eight weeks, and was respected by his coworkers. The former Chicago police officer arrived in Wichita about a year prior and walked the far eastern beat on Douglas Avenue. Patrolman Fenner described Kerwin's attitude as very happy and talkative during the morning before the accident, when the two responded to a report of a man burying a dead animal. His last act of duty was the arrest of a man for drunkenness along East Douglas Avenue.

With the coroner being out of town, Justice Barrett arrived on scene at 1100 hours to a room full of acquaintances and fellow officers; the late John W. Kerwin unmoved from where he collapsed. The inquest began after a jury was summoned to the scene, which consisted of W. B. Jones, A. T. Buckridge, A. Knowles, J. C. Boyman, O. O. Oliver, and E. F. McNeill.

William Christianson was the first to testify. He indicated that Kerwin was inside the store inspecting a revolver he wanted in exchange for his duty weapon. Mr. Christianson agreed to the trade with Kerwin, which the latter turned and drew his revolver to show the former. During the presentation of his pistol is when the shot was fired, and when Kerwin fell to the floor, bellowing, "Oh, my God!" When the firearm was discharged, Christianson became startled and believed he was the one struck by the round.

Saul Miller, a citizen, was the next man to testify, specifying that he was first to arrive at the incident location after Kerwin was shot. Christianson, at the time, told Miller the same account of events upon his arrival as he testified to the jury and judge. Kerwin's body remained in the same position when officers arrived on scene as when Miller first saw him; arms extended, and a .38 caliber revolver on the floor next to him.

Patrolman Fenner testified under oath after Miller. Fenner and Kerwin became friends quickly after Kerwin joined the force, which was fifty-two days prior to the incident. Fenner indicated he never heard Kerwin make any suicidal statements and possessed a sprightly and positive personality.[2]

At that time, a heartrending scene unfolded when Mrs. Kerwin entered the store and hurried to the body of her late husband with tears streaming from her eyes. It took some time for friends to convince Mrs. Kerwin to leave her dead husband's side and

---

2. "Through the Heart," *The Wichita Beacon,* March 23, 1888.

return home. Understandably, the room was filled with sadness by sympathetic friends and acquaintances of the deceased. After Mrs. Kerwin was escorted from the room, the hearing moved forward. Additional witnesses testified, but nothing of substance was heard that was not already mentioned.

Dr. H. C. Hood, the final witness, indicated he examined the body right after Kerwin died, and that the round entered his chest, near the center, in a downward angle through the heart. The death of Kerwin was immediate.

The one question that concerned the jury was why the bullet entered high on the chest and angled downward if the revolver was drawn from Kerwin's side. The jury concluded that his intent was to extract the bullets from the gun before showing it to the proprietor. Ultimately, it was decided that Kerwin died by an accidental gunshot wound fired by his own hand.[3]

Fellow officers of Kerwin raised a generous sum of money for the widow and her family after Kerwin's death.[4] The entire police department and the Kansas National Guard conducted a military burial for the slain officer in the Catholic cemetery.[5]

---

3. "Through the Heart," *The Wichita Beacon*, March 23, 1888.

4. "A Benefit," *The Wichita Beacon*, March 24, 1888.

5. "Policeman's *[sic]* Kerwin's Funeral," *The Wichita Beacon*, March 24, 1888.

2

PATROLMAN HENRY EBENHACK

Date: September 24, 1888
Day: Monday
Time: 0700 hours
Location: 1st Street and Market Street
Tour: Ten months
Age: Twenty-eight
Race: White
Gender: Male
Marital Status: Married
Military Veteran: Yes
Children: One[1]
Badge: Not applicable
Burial: Highland Cemetery, Wichita, Sedgwick County, Kansas
Cause: Gunfire
Weapon: Revolver
Offender Status: Convicted of second-degree manslaughter
Offender Age: Unknown
Offender Race: White
Offender Gender: Male
City Marshal at the Time: Thomas McNamara

---

1. "Brutal Murder," *The Wichita Weekly Journal*, September 27, 1888. Ebenhack buried an adopted child about one week before his murder.

On the morning of Monday, September 24, 1888, Patrolman Henry Ebenhack, of the Wichita Police Department (also referred to as the Metropolitan Police at the time), was shot and killed by John Thornton, of McMahan's Patrol.

Patrolman Ebenhack, along with Patrolman Hartzell, walked to a bawdy house at 456 North Main Street between 0600 hours and 0700 hours, where they believed Thornton was present. Ebenhack believed Thorton was involved in illegal activity at the house where prostitutes worked.

McMahan's Patrol was a private company established in Wichita in July of 1888.[2] The patrol was paid by area merchants to protect their properties. Their services consisted of the use of alarm and signal boxes that were installed on both sides of Main Street between English Street and 2nd Street, as well as Douglas Avenue from the bridge to Fifth Avenue (called Santa Fe Avenue today). *The Wichita Daily Eagle* described the newly formed patrolmen: "With one exception they are all big six footers, but the exception makes up in other ways what he lacks in height. Each man wears a regulation policeman's dark blue uniform with brass buttons. The helmet is a regulation black helmet, on the front of this is 'McMahan's Patrol,' in silver letters. The club is about two feet in length and worn in a belt." [3]

Upon arrival at the brothel, Hartzell knocked on the front door while Ebenhack waited at the rear door. Thornton, who was in his uniform, opened the front door. Ebenhack walked back around the house to the front and placed Thornton under arrest. Thornton indicated he was at the house on business for McMahan, but Ebenhack did not believe him and informed Thornton that he would have to explain his actions in court.

As the three started walking down the street, Ebenhack and Thornton side-by-side, while Hartzell was behind them, Thornton stated that Ebenhack had it in for him, and the two began to argue with each other. They walked south to 2nd Street, and then east, passing the Christian church on Market Street, when Thornton pushed up his coat sleeves and said they would "fight it out." In response, Ebenhack hit him with a light whip handle in the head.[4]

---

2. "McMahan's Patrol," *The Wichita Beacon*, July 16, 1888.

3. "The McMahan Patrol," *The Wichita Eagle*, July 21, 1888.

4. "Shot Dead," *The Wichita Eagle*, September 25, 1888.

Hartzell grabbed Thornton around the waist and attempted to break up the fight, but Thornton reached into his pocket and drew a revolver. It is believed the first shot that Thornton fired struck Ebenhack in the chest, causing him to reel backward. Ebenhack reached for the revolver in his own hip pocket while Thornton fired again, grazing Ebenhack's coat. The third shot missed and struck a house across the street. Ebenhack stumbled backward and fell into the middle of the street. Thornton handed over his two revolvers to Hartzell and told him that he was ready to die. Hartzell then escorted him to the city jail.

Several citizens that were nearby witnessed the commotion and carried Ebenhack to the engine house where he quietly expired. The body was then escorted to his former home at 618 South Market Street.

Coroner Percy was informed of the killing and had Deputy Metcalf summon a jury, which consisted of J. G. McCoy, George Litzenberg, George Pray, William S. Cotter, John Herrig, and L. Simpson. The inquest was set for 1300 hours. Justice Walker saw Thornton in his court and continued his preliminary hearing to October 12. Thornton's attorneys consisted of Mr. Dale, Mr. Wall, Judge J. R. Shields, and E. M. Cochran.

The coroner and jury observed the remains at 618 South Market Street. Afterward, they went to the coroner's office at the courthouse, which was surrounded by curious citizens. J. W. Adams represented the state, and upon his arrival, the inquest began with Hartzell's testimony without the prisoner present.[5]

Hartzell's testimony with Mr. Adams consisted of the following:

> I have been a policeman for about seven months; was acquainted with [sic] deceased; he was on the force before I was; I am, too, acquainted with Mr. Thornton and have been for five months. About half past 6 I was coming down from breakfast on a street car, when Ebenhack motioned me to come to him. I did so and he asked me to go up to the corner of Central and Main and "pull" John Thornton, who was "laying up" with one of the women in the room (pointing to one of two who had been summoned into court as witnesses.) We went to the house and I went to the front door and Henry to the back door. I knocked on [sic] front door and found Thornton in the room when it was opened. I called

---

5. "Shot Dead," *The Wichita Eagle,* September 25, 1888.

Henry to come around; he came and said to Thornton, "I want you." Thornton said, "I came here on business for McMahan." When he and Ebenhack started down town to the police station he said Henry had it in for him and began talking and continued telling what he could do with Henry until we got to the corner of First and Market, just past the Christian church, when Thornton said "I can do you," and turned half around, facing the west, and began rolling up his sleeves. Henry struck at Thornton with a light whip handle and hit him on the shoulder or the face, don't know exactly which. I grabbed hold of him around the waist but somehow he got his revolver out of his pocket and commenced firing. He fired three shots; the first seemed to take effect for Henry reeled back and put his hand as if to feel for his gun. Then followed the second and third shots, Henry getting each time further from Thornton until at the last shot he staggered and fell almost in the middle of the street. After he had shot Ebenhack he handed me his gun, saying: "Here is my gun, and I have another." He then reached into his pocket and pulled out a second revolver, and I gave them to Knight. . . . I said then you have killed him and it will go hard with you. He said, well I am ready to die.[6]

During cross-examination, Hartzell indicated that Ebenhack told him that he was going to arrest Thornton and never mentioned that he had it out for him. Hartzell said they had no warrant for Thornton, and that he was not sure if Ebenhack cursed at Thornton while he was making the arrest. He then mentioned that making arrests without warrants was common, and he did not know if Ebenhack was armed with a gun or just the whip. Hartzell claimed they all knew that Thornton had made a report to the police commissioners about Patrolman Fenner going into a house of prostitution, and that Charley Dixon, a citizen, was the first person he saw on scene after the shooting.

Patrolman John Knight saw the three men walking down Market Street as he was headed to the station just before the shooting. Charles Dixon was on the other side of the street from Knight, and both gave alike accounts of what they saw, which was very similar to Hartzell's account.

---

6. "Shot Dead," *The Wichita Eagle*, September 25, 1888.

A city physician, Dr. McClees, examined the body soon after the shooting, observing that one shot entered the left breast, approximately two inches above the nipple, passing through the heart. Alf Brownell, who was a member of Hose Company No. 1 from the local fire house, knew both Ebenhack and Thornton, and first saw them walking toward the engine house. The men stopped and Ebenhack beat Thornton over the head, and then a shot went off. Hartzell was holding Thornton, who reached around Hartzell and shot Ebenhack.[7]

Nora Medsgar, a female who presumably worked at the house in an unspecified capacity, was the first witness to testify after the jury reconvened, indicating that Ebenhack arrived at the house around 0700 hours. Medsgar claimed she did not see Thornton prior to observing Ebenhack, originally thinking that the two arrived at the location together. During examination, Medsgar told the county attorney that Thornton walked to the front door, and Hartzell (not Ebenhack) said, "Come out here, I want you. . . . Come and go along with me."[8]

Upon cross-examination by Mr. Dall, Medsgar specified that Thornton came to her room around 0630 hours, and Ebenhack arrived at 0640 hours, which was inconsistent with her earlier statement. The first officer she saw was Hartzell as he was looking through the window. At this time, Thornton, who was dressed, was sitting on the end of her bed. Hartzell knocked on the front door and someone opened it, followed by Hartzell exclaiming, "Come out, I want you." In response, Thornton walked to the porch and asked, "What do you want?" Hartzell called for Ebenhack, and Ebenhack told Thornton to "Come along." Medsgar did not hear an altercation before the three left the house.[9]

Lewis Clark, who testified next, said he was sixty to seventy yards away when he observed Hartzell and Thornton in a physical struggle, when Thornton reached around Hartzell to shoot Ebenhack. After the shooting, Ebenhack "staggered" into the street and fell to the ground. Hartzell and Thornton were standing on the sidewalk, and Ebenhack was next to it with one of his feet on the edge, about six to eight feet away from the two. It did not appear the second shot struck Ebenhack, and when the third shot was fired, a small piece of Ebenhack's coat flew. The third shot, according to Clark, was not deadly because Ebenhack fell a few seconds after it was fired. Ebenhack fell on his right arm and

---

7. "Shot Dead," *The Wichita Eagle*, September 25, 1888.

8. "The Coroner's Verdict," *The Wichita Eagle*, September 26, 1888.

9. "Coroner's Verdict," *Wichita Eagle*.

then rolled onto his face. The time in between shots was a few seconds, and Ebenhack had a "billy" in one of his hands. Hartzell looked over his shoulder as Thornton fired the shots and had his arm around the shooter.

The next to testify was Warren McKee, a member of Hose Company No. 1, who knew both Ebenhack and Thornton. McKee was on his way to the engine house from the boarding house, the latter located at 2nd Street and Main Street. Ebenhack struck Thornton two or three times, and Hartzell intervened by getting between the two. Thornton reached into his pocket and shot around Hartzell at Ebenhack, causing one arm to raise up upon impact. As Thornton continued shooting, Ebenhack stumbled backward. McKee said he saw the pistol just before or right at the same time Hartzell grabbed Thornton. Ebenhack tried to strike Thornton over Hartzell's shoulder when Thornton pulled out the revolver. When the first shot was fired, the two men were four feet apart and Ebenhack was on the sidewalk.

During the cross-examination, McKee said Ebenhack condemned Thornton for talking badly about him. McKee knew nothing about any hostility between the police and McMahan's Patrol. He believed Hartzell saw the gun coming out of Thornton's pocket, so Hartzell grabbed him. McKee again confirmed the three were on the sidewalk when the first shot was fired, and it was the first shot that was most likely deadly.

John A. Davidson, who was familiar with both men, was aware of some friction between the two. On Thursday, prior to the incident, around 1730 hours, Davidson was standing at Lawrence Avenue (called Broadway Avenue today) and Douglas Avenue when Ebenhack contacted him, asking him to go to the Stem building. Ebenhack made a comment that a couple of people he did not like were there. After they arrived, Davidson saw Thornton and Charley Long there, so he and Ebenhack went to a back room and talked for a while, then left. It is unknown if Charley Long was a co-worker of Thornton's or was a citizen.

A couple of hours later, as Davidson was in front of the Zimmerly building, Thornton approached him and said, "I want to see you. If you have any friends who have anything against me, tell them they want to come fixed, for if they don't I will sure fix them." Davidson informed Thornton that he knew of no problems. Thornton said he saw Davidson with Ebenhack earlier, and Davidson asked Thornton if he meant Ebenhack in particular. Thornton replied that he did not. Davidson curiously asked

Thornton what the issue was. Thornton replied, "We keep those girls and don't want anyone monkeying around there."[10]

Davidson indicated Ebenhack made a statement that he would someday catch the men, and the women that the men were "laying up with." He also said that Thornton had reported Ebenhack and Patrolman Fenner multiple times, and that he would get even. It is unknown what Thornton reported Ebenhack and Fenner for. Davidson went out to measure the sidewalk where the shooting took place, learning that it was 5 feet and 3.75 inches wide.

McMahan was summoned to testify next, and he described the duties of his patrolmen. The patrol was expected to visit prostitution houses to find evidence of any wrongdoing, and they should have been familiar with those on their beat that were suspected criminals. The patrolmen and the Metropolitan police officers had a good working relationship. McMahan's patrolmen were sworn in by the police commissioners, same as the regular police were, and all their arrested subjects were turned over to the regular police.

Nora Medsgar was recalled and explained that Thornton had been to the house two or three times in the past. The previous morning, Thornton visited them to talk about a house and its location that they asked him to rent for them. This was the sole topic that was discussed during the contact.

After the testimony, the jury deliberated for two hours and returned the following verdict: "An inquisition holden at Wichita City, Sedgwick county [*sic*], Kan., on the 24th and 25th days of September, 1888, before me, O. F. Pearcey, coroner of Sedgwick county [*sic*], on the dead body of Henry Ebenhack, there lying dead, by the jurors whose names are hereunto subscribed. The said jurors, upon their oaths, do say that from the testimony given the deceased came to his death from a gunshot wound at the hands of one John Thornton, on the 24th day of September, 1888, and we further find that said shot was fired without felonious intent, but under great provocation and danger of bodily injury."[11]

Of the six jurors, all of them knew Ebenhack and three of them were personal friends of his; none were acquainted with Thornton.

After the testimony, none of them believed Thornton was guilty of murdering Ebenhack. Through interviews with jury members, it was discovered they believed Eben-

---

10. "The Coroner's Verdict," *The Wichita Eagle*, September 26, 1888.

11. "Coroner's Verdict," *Wichita Eagle*.

hack should have never arrested Thornton; the arrest most likely was a way for Ebenhack to discredit him. If there was no tension between the two men, the arrest most likely would not have occurred and Thornton's entrance into the bawdy house would have been perceived as part of his work duties. The jury believed that Ebenhack was a good and brave officer, but he made a mistake on September 24, 1888, and paid for it with his life.[12]

However, prosecutors decided to take the matter to court, and on the morning of October 4, 1888, Thornton was brought into Justice Walker's courtroom in reference to his preliminary hearing. Hartzell was called to the stand and cross-examined by the defense, testifying with little to no difference from the coroner's inquest. Attorneys Mr. Dale and Mr. Shields argued for the dismissal of the case against Thornton, but he was bound over on the charge of first-degree murder. Since the "proof of the crime (was) not evident, nor the presumption great," his bail was set at $2,000, which he later secured.[13]

Thornton's trial for murder in the first degree was held in January of 1889 in Judge Reed's courtroom. County attorneys Jones, John W. Adams, and A. R. Museller prosecuted for the state, while Thornton was defended by Judge Shields, Judge F. P. Martin, and T. F. McMeacham.[14]

Thornton was ultimately convicted of manslaughter in the second degree and sentenced to three years in Leavenworth on April 9, 1889. When asked for any reason why he should not have received the punishment imposed, Thornton calmly said that he had no complaints but believed he was acting in self-defense.[15]

Both men involved in the deadly altercation had the respect of many citizens and the officers they served with.

Ebenhack grew up on the cattle range and was considered an expert shot and rider. He had married shortly before his death and was twenty-eight years old.

Thornton was often described as a good-looking and quiet man, who served on the St. Louis Police Department before moving to Wichita.[16]

---

12. "The Coroner's Verdict," *The Wichita Eagle*, September 26, 1888.

13. "Released on Bond," *The Wichita Beacon*, October 4, 1888.

14. "State Vs. Thornton," *The Wichita Eagle,* January 10, 1889.

15. "State Vs. Thornton," *The Wichita Eagle*, April 10, 1889.

16. "Shot Dead," *The Wichita Eagle*, September 25, 1888.

3

PATROLMAN S. A. HARTZELL

Date: December 14, 1888
Day: Incident occurred on Thursday - Died on Friday
Time: Incident occurred at 1100 hours - Died at 0630 hours
Location: Chicago Avenue (now Douglas Avenue)
Tour: Ten months (1888)
Age: Forty-four
Race: White
Gender: Male
Marital Status: Married
Military Veteran: Yes - Army - Civil War
Children: Six
Badge: Not applicable
Burial: Highland Cemetery, Wichita, Sedgwick County, Kansas
Cause: Gunfire (accidental)
Weapon: .38 caliber revolver
Offender Status: Not applicable
Offender Age: Not applicable
Offender Race: Not applicable
Offender Gender: Not applicable
City Marshal at the Time: Thomas McNamara

Patrolman S. A. Hartzell's Grave Marker. November 23, 2024. Taken by Christopher P. Marceau.

Patrolman S. A. Hartzell, a popular police officer, was accidentally shot by E. E. Blood on Thursday, December 13, 1888, shortly before 1100 hours at a second-hand store called Turner and Blood, which was located on Chicago Avenue (now Douglas Avenue). Hartzell wanted to trade his .38 caliber revolver for a different one with a shorter barrel that would fit better in his pocket.

Upon entering the store, Hartzell asked Blood, "Well, are you ready to make that trade?" Blood located the gun on a nearby shelf and gave it to the officer. Hartzell transferred the bullets from his old gun to his new one and placed the weapon in his inside coat pocket.[1]

While talking with the officer, Blood wanted to show him some things about the weapon, so the gun was handed back to Blood. Unaware that Hartzell placed cartridges in the revolver, while demonstrating the difficulty of pulling back the hammer, Blood's finger slipped, and a bullet was discharged into Hartzell's body. Hartzell yelled, "See

---

1. "Fatal Accident," *The Wichita Eagle*, December 14, 1888.

what you have done!" As Hartzell walked toward the front door of the business, another individual asked him if he was shot. Hartzell responded, "Yes, it was entirely accidental; don't blame Blood."[2]

Hartzell was taken next door to J. G. Booth & Co.'s, where he lay down on a cot. Dr. Oldham was fetched by a citizen and discovered an entry wound to Hartzell's left side, approximately two inches below his heart. Even with the assistance of Dr. Jordon, the two doctors were unable to locate the ball.

Hartzell's wife and fellow officers tended to him until the evening, when he was moved to a room at the Riverside Hotel on the opposite side of the river. Several doctors, including Purdy, Oldham, Fabrique, Jordon, Hinsdale, and Hoffman, attempted to locate the projectile but were unsuccessful. They concluded the wound would eventually cause death.

At 0200 hours, surgery commenced and revealed the ball had traveled below the seventh rib and downwards through the stomach. It ultimately came to rest in a back muscle after it severed multiple arteries. The surgical procedure was terminated, confirming that the wound would prove fatal.[3]

Hartzell died on Friday, December 14, 1888, between 0600 hours and 0700 hours, at the hotel. His remains were taken to his family's home at 840 Wabash Avenue the following afternoon. An inquest was held at 1400 hours by the coroner, with a present jury. Dr. Oldham was the first witness to testify, and said the following:

> I was called December 13, at 10:30 I think, to West Wichita. I found [*sic*] deceased lying in a store and was suffering very severely from a shock; did not examine [*sic*] wound at that time as I wanted to bring about a reaction. I saw him again at 2 o'clock. Dr. Jordon was with me and I saw his condition was much the same. He had vomited clotted blood; thought that it came from the stomach. I saw him again at 5 and 6; indication of reaction; extremities warm; saw him again at 7. Dr. Fabrique and I thought then an examination only could do; called in Jordon, Purdy, Hinsdale and Hoffman. We opened the abdominal cavity [*sic*] saw large quantity of blood in same. We secured bleeding points and sewed up [*sic*]

---

2. "Fatal Accident," *The Wichita Eagle*, December 14, 1888.

3. "Fatal Accident," *Wichita Eagle*.

wound in stomach, saw that the ball had passed through the stomach and cut the spinal arteries; wound was necessarily fatal. I heard Hartzell say the shot was purely accidental and that he did not want Blood prosecuted; he was at the time perfectly rational.[4]

The next witness to testify was W. D. Turner, who said the following:

About 10 o'clock Hartzell came into our store and said he wanted to trade off his pistol. My partner, E. Blood, said all right, and then he showed his pistol. I told him to trade for $1 or even. I came to see he had traded to us. Blood said let me see [sic] pistol I traded you; Hartzell handed it to him. When Blood had [sic] pistol in his hand it went off. Then I heard Blood say, "are you hurt?" Hartzell replied: "My God, man; see what you have done?" and he walked out to the sidewalk. Then he said it is but a mere accident, and went into Booth's store. I did not hear exactly what Blood did say when he took the revolver, but think he said let me show you something about it; think that it would not go off at half-cock. It was a 38 British bull-dog. Hartzell and Blood were both good friends; Hartzell would come into the store two or three times a day.[5]

J. R. Booth indicated the following:

Yesterday I started from my store on the West Side to come over the river. Just as I took hold of the door I heard a shot; I heard some one [sic] say I am shot or killed; I went in front of the second hand store and saw Hartzell with his hand on his side and in distress. Blood said, "what have I done?" Hartzell started for my door and I got a cot ready for him; I put him upon the cot and telephoned the police headquarters; I went to Hartzell and thought he was dying; I said tell me all about it and he related how he had traded and then Blood said, "let me show you something in

---

4. "The Inquest," *The Wichita Eagle*, December 15, 1888.

5. "Inquest," *Wichita Eagle*.

regard to the gun." The boy let it go off accidentally. He stated positively that it was an accident. I told the crowd what he said and Hartzell said "yes;" he said telephone for my wife. I heard him say several times that he did not want him prosecuted.[6]

C. A. Marford said the following:

I was at Turner and Blood's store the morning of December 13th and Hartzell came in; wanted to trade guns for $1 or even. They traded, I don't know how, I went to [sic] front and Turner looked at [sic] pistol he had traded for; put [sic] in his pocket and asked Hartzell if he could carry; he thought not. Blood took it and said let me show you something. It exploded; did not think there was a loaded gun in the house. Hartzell put his hand to his side, walked to the side-walk and exclaimed: "Boys it is an accident. Hartzell said, "don't let him hurt himself (referring to Blood). I saw blood on Hartzell when he was in Booth's store.[7]

The citizens of the jury were John Fisher, T. Lilly, V. A. Haynes, J. W. Huston, W. P. Mosley, and A. H. McKee. Their verdict read the following: "The deceased came to his death from a pistol shot wound at the hands of E. E. Blood, and we, the jury, further find that the shooting was accidental and that the said E. E. Blood is fully exonerated from blame."[8]

The funeral was held the following Sunday. *The Wichita Daily Eagle* noted that Blood became nearly insane because of the accident.

Hartzell had been with the Department for about ten months when he was killed. Citizens perceived him as being honest and fair and always arrested the man he was after. He was forty-four years old and the father of six children. Born in Perry County, Ohio, in 1843, he enlisted in the 7th Ohio Regiment, Company G, at the start of the Civil War, and mustered out near the end of it. Hartzell was buried in Highland Cemetery. E. E. Blood

---

6. "The Inquest," *The Wichita Eagle*, December 15, 1888.

7. "Inquest," *Wichita Eagle*.

8. "Inquest," *Wichita Eagle*.

was twenty-three years old at the time of the incident and came from a family of farmers a few miles south of Wichita.[9]

---

9. "Police Officer Hartzell, of Wichita, Accidentally Shot and Killed Last Thursday," *The Mocking Bird*, December 22, 1888.

PART TWO

FIFTEEN OFFICERS IN SIXTEEN YEARS: THE RISE OF SUBSTANCE ABUSE, GANGSTERS, AND AUTOMOBILES

4

DETECTIVE WILLIAM L. HUMPHRIES

Date: February 23, 1915
Day: Tuesday
Time: Approximately 1500 hours
Location: 806 East Douglas Avenue
Tour: Two years, four months (October 1912 to February 1915)
Age: Forty
Race: White
Gender: Male
Marital Status: Married
Military Veteran: Unknown
Children: One
Badge: Not applicable
Burial: Maple Grove Cemetery, Wichita, Sedgwick County, Kansas
Cause: Gunfire
Weapon: Colt .38 Special revolver
Offender Status: Convicted of murder
Offender Age: Thirty-six
Offender Race: White
Offender Gender: Male
Chief of Police at the Time: G. C. Kensler

Detective William L. Humphries. The Wichita Beacon. February 24, 1915. Public Domain.

Detective William L. Humphries was shot and killed by Auda M. "Audie" Caplinger on Tuesday, February 23, 1915. The incident occurred in Jim Quick's Pool Hall, which was located at 806 East Douglas Avenue.[1] The victim in this case was considered the chief of Wichita's detectives, although Humphries did not prefer this honor as his official title. "Detective," simply put, was his preference. The Wichita Police Department hired the humble man in October 1912. One of Humphries' previous jobs was Chief of Police in Ouray, Colorado.[2]

Patrons of the pool hall knew the suspect as "Tracy." He was known for carrying a gun and had displayed it before the murder.

In the afternoon on the day of the incident, the detective made a round to the pool halls on East Douglas Avenue. When Humphries first ran into Caplinger in the Quick Pool Hall, Caplinger was extremely intoxicated. The unpretentious detective told Caplinger, "I feel sorry for you and do not want to arrest you, but I am going to put you

---

1. "Humphries Shot to Death While Making an Arrest," *The Wichita Beacon*, February 23, 1915.

2. "Gun Toting and Alcohol Blamed for the Shooting," *The Wichita Beacon*, February 24, 1915.

out of the hall and I do not want you to come back till you are sober."[3] Caplinger was then escorted out of the hall, and the detective left on foot.

Not long after, Humphries participated in some shooting practice at the Forum with fellow officers C. E. Galloway, W. A. McWain, and Jack Hay. Then he went to City Hall and placed his revolver and holster in his locker because it was hurting his side. He left City Hall and walked to Union Station where he met up with Patrolman Morgan, who was preparing to inspect passengers getting off the train at 1505 hours. Humphries mentioned to Morgan that his revolver was hurting his side, and that he was unarmed. He took off walking eastbound on Douglas Avenue and was near the pool hall when a barber named S. W. Larson yelled at him for his assistance.[4]

D. C. Crabb, a carpenter, was a witness to the shooting of Humphries. According to Crabb, when he went into the pool hall late in the afternoon, Auda M. Caplinger was still there. The inebriated Caplinger must have re-entered the business after the detective had left. Crabb, who knew Caplinger, observed him messing with his gun while indicating he was going to "make a smoke."[5] Crabb told Caplinger not to.

According to Crabb, Caplinger informed him that he would leave the pool hall if Crabb went with him. Crabb walked with the befuddled Caplinger toward the front door. While on the way, Caplinger still had the gun in his hand and discharged a round into the floor. Around that time is when Humphries was walking close to the pool hall and Larson beckoned him. Caplinger became aware of the detective's presence and attempted to escape through the back door.[6]

The detective pursued Caplinger, who warned Humphries to stay back or he would shoot him. Humphries disregarded the threat and continued to approach Caplinger, who fired a shot that missed the detective. Another shot was fired and struck the detective in the head, causing him to fall to his hasty death.

Crabb, who was present during the shooting, grabbed Caplinger from behind and wrestled with him, despite Caplinger's threats to kill him. Crabb was able to place a finger in the trigger guard and prevented the gun from being fired. Also nearby was Larson, who

---

3. "Gun Toting and Alcohol Blamed for the Shooting," *The Wichita Beacon*, February 24, 1915.

4. "Kills Detective Who Tries to Arrest Him," *The Wichita Eagle*, February 24, 1915.

5. "Gun Toting," *Wichita Beacon*.

6. "Gun Toting," *Wichita Beacon*.

assisted Crabb with the restraint of the suspect. The remaining men in the pool hall, who most likely became fearful of the unfolding event, left after the first shot.

It was later discovered that the bullet had entered the right side of Detective Humphries' head and lodged in his brain.[7]

A bottle of "White Mule," which is a mixture of alcohol and water, was taken off Caplinger after he was arrested.[8] Caplinger was eventually taken to the police station where he refused to give officers a statement. Officers learned that the gun used by the suspect was a Colt .38 Special revolver.[9]

The funeral for Detective Humphries was held on the following Thursday after the shooting.[10] The entire department attended the funeral service with hundreds of others, including citizens, firefighters, and city officials. Not everyone could fit inside the Gill Funeral Home. Chief G. C. Kensler attended and was at the front of his men.[11] The forty-five men of the Wichita Police Department wore crepe bands on their arms during mourning.[12]

Later, Caplinger was tried in Judge Thornton W. Sargent's court room in district court. The prosecutor for this case was County Attorney Ross McCormick, and defending Auda M. Caplinger was D. O. Potts. D. O. Potts claimed Caplinger had no memory of killing Humphries due to his level of intoxication, thus, he was hoping for a verdict of third-degree manslaughter.[13]

Caplinger was convicted of first-degree murder on November 12, 1915.[14] This was not Caplinger's first murder conviction. Several years before the Quick Pool Hall

---

7. "Gun Toting and Alcohol Blamed for the Shooting," *The Wichita Beacon*, February 24, 1915.

8. "A Bottle of Alcohol Taken Off Caplinger," *The Wichita Beacon*, February 24, 1915.

9. "Humphries Shot to Death While Making an Arrest," *The Wichita Beacon*, February 23, 1915. After the shooting, a card was located by an officer in Caplinger's pocket that read "A. M. Kaplinger, 1003 East Douglas Avenue. In case of accident notify Mrs. Callie Kaplinger."

10. "Gun Toting," *Wichita Beacon*. At the time Detective Humphries was killed, he had $1635 in life and accident insurance.

11. "Chapel Too Small for the Mourners," *The Wichita Beacon*, February 26, 1915.

12. "Police in Mourning for the Dead Officer," *The Wichita Beacon*, February 24, 1915.

13. "A Murder or Manslaughter," *The Wichita Beacon*, November 10, 1915.

14. "First Degree, Their Verdict," *The Wichita Beacon*, November 12, 1915.

incident, Caplinger was convicted of killing a black person in Camden, Arkansas. While his sentence was two years, he only served two months in an Arkansas penitentiary.[15]

An interesting discovery about this case, which occurred during prohibition in Kansas, was Mary Caplinger, the mother of Auda M. Caplinger, who filed a lawsuit after the murder in the amount of $10,000 against Omie Davis, a druggist.

Omie Davis allegedly sold Caplinger the alcohol that made him intoxicated and was, according to Mary, the cause of his homicidal behavior. The suit also named Fern F. Jordan, the owner of the building that housed Davis's business.[16] The plaintiff claimed that Auda Caplinger would not have committed the crime if he had been sober. The lawsuit also alleged that because her son was serving time in a penitentiary, he could not support her. Surprisingly, the jury awarded Mary Caplinger $500 in damages.[17]

Humphries resided at 1100 South Lawrence Avenue. He was survived by his wife and child.[18]

---

15. "Gun Toting and Alcohol Blamed for the Shooting," *The Wichita Beacon*, February 24, 1915.

16. "Mother Sues Druggist," *Meade County News*, March 18, 1915.

17. "Selling of Liquor Costs Davis $500," *The Wichita Eagle*, June 30, 1917.

18. "Humphries Shot to Death While Making an Arrest," *The Wichita Beacon*, February 23, 1915.

5

Captain Frank W. Griswold

Date: May 23, 1915
Day: Sunday
Time: After 0100 hours
Location: 228 North Main Street
Tour: Six years (1909-1915)
Age: Fifty-six
Race: White
Gender: Male
Marital Status: Married
Military Veteran: Unknown
Children: Large family
Badge: Not applicable
Burial: Maple Grove Cemetery, Wichita, Sedgwick County, Kansas
Cause: Gunfire
Weapon: Gun - Unknown type
Offender Status: Never convicted
Offender Age: Unknown
Offender Race: Unknown
Offender Gender: Unknown
Chief of Police at the Time: O. K. Stewart

Captain Frank W. Griswold. The Wichita Eagle. May 25, 1915. Public Domain.

Exactly three months after the death of Detective William L. Humphries, another calamity struck the Wichita Police Department. On Sunday, May 23, 1915, shortly after 0100 hours, Captain Frank W. Griswold was shot in the head and near the heart by burglars at 228 North Main Street.[1] Griswold was born in Hamilton, Illinois on October 20, 1858, and moved to Wichita seven years before his death.[2] Patrolman Allen Harrell was also shot in the right arm after the two officers surprised the burglars, who were stealing from the A. E. Bump shoe store.[3]

---

1. "Wichita Police Captain Killed in Gun Battle," *The Wichita Eagle*, May 23, 1915.

2. "Not Sure Burglars Mexicans," *The Wichita Eagle*, May 25, 1915.

3. "Captain Killed," *Wichita Eagle*.

The Britton Barbers' Supply Store, at 238 North Main Street, was a victim of a burglary that occurred the previous Thursday. Mr. Tierney and his wife lived above the supply store. Shortly before the murder of Captain Griswold, they heard someone trying to break into the supply store, so they called the police. After hearing about the call, Patrolman Al Harrell contacted the Tierney's in person.

The husband and wife informed the officer that they observed three men who looked like "Mexicans" in the alley behind the store. They could hear the use of keys at the back door. The Tierney's believed the suspects noticed the light in their apartment, which may have caused the suspects to leave. Harrell checked the back alley and observed a hole that had been cut in the rear door of the Bump shoe store.

According to Harrell, the hole was large enough for a person to reach through and lift the security bar protecting the door. Harrell later indicated that the bar was still up, but it seemed suspicious to him. Harrell decided to make a call at a nearby livery stable for additional officers. Captain Griswold and Special Officer Cruse arrived at the location, and they went to the back door. Harrell briefed the captain on the information the Tierney's told him. The captain told Cruse to go around the building and monitor the front door.

Harrell later indicated he reached inside the hole and took down the bar while simultaneously holding his flashlight between his legs. Harrell dropped the flashlight. The captain, who did not have a flashlight with him, picked up Harrell's light. Regrettably for the captain, the possession of this flashlight may have been a causative factor in his murder that occurred a short time later. Harrell was the first to enter the store, with the captain immediately behind him.

After entering the business, Harrell saw a nearby door to a bathroom swing almost shut. He tried to push the door open, but it struck a man that was hiding behind it. The man fired a shot through the door at Harrell that missed him. After the shot, the door opened, and Harrell observed what he believed at the time to be a short Hispanic male with what appeared to be a .32 caliber Smith and Wesson. Harrell moved to the west while simultaneously pointing his gun at the door. He gave the burglar a command to come out, but there was no response.[4]

---

4. "Burglars, Trapped in Store Slay Police Captain; Escape," *The Wichita Beacon*, May 24, 1915.

According to Harrell, Captain Griswold ordered, "Come on out and come with your hands up."[5] The suspect replied that he was coming out. Harrell informed the suspect that he had one second to exit the bathroom, and when the male did not respond, Harrell fired a shot into the room. In response, the suspect fired back through the crack in the door where he was hiding behind.

The captain moved behind Harrell while contemporaneously firing toward the suspect. The suspect fired back again, leaving Harrell between the lines of fire. The captain utilized Harrell's flashlight in an attempt to illuminate the threat. A bullet then pierced Harrell's right arm from behind him. Harrell later specified that he was not sure if the round came from Griswold's gun, or from an additional suspect who was to the south of them.

Captain Griswold informed Harrell that he was hit and started for the front door. As he reached the center of the room, he said, "I'm done for, Al," and fell to the ground. According to Harrell, those were his last words. Harrell's shattered gun arm was to his side and inoperative.[6]

Cruse remained at the front door during the gunfight. Just after he looked through the front window, a bullet came crashing through it.[7] To escape the chaotic scene, Harrell kicked out the front glass window and crawled through it to Cruse. Assisted by Cruse, Harrell then went to Ed Kessler's place across the street.[8] Harrell informed Cruse that Captain Griswold was still inside and down, and he eventually went to the hospital.[9]

Numerous officers and civilians arrived at the scene several minutes later, and it was not until half an hour later that officers would re-enter the store for fear that the suspects were still hiding inside. Patrolman Murrel, Patrolman Bish, and Assistant Chief of Police Jack Hay entered the store and realized the heartbreaking death of the captain.

It was discovered that the burglars must have made their escape through the unguarded rear door of the business. Neighbors, who resided in rooms above the shoe store, heard three men running in the alley after the shooting. After learning the killers

---

5. "Burglars, Trapped in Store Slay Police Captain; Escape," *The Wichita Beacon*, May 24, 1915.

6. "Burglars," *Wichita Beacon*.

7. "Wichita Police Captain Killed in Gun Battle," *The Wichita Eagle*, May 23, 1915.

8. "Burglars," *Wichita Beacon*.

9. "Captain Killed," *Wichita Eagle*.

escaped, Chief of Police O. K. Stewart called into action the entire police force to round up "every suspicious character in the city." The Sedgwick County Sheriff's Office joined in the search for the slayers.[10]

Griswold's lifeless body was found lying on his back in the middle of the shoe store; his police hat was still on his head, a revolver in one hand and an operational flashlight in the other. He sustained two gunshot wounds, one to his left breast and another behind his right ear. Blood was streaming from his mouth. A ten-foot trail of blood led to a cellar door from the captain.

It was believed that Captain Griswold died fighting; evidenced by the three empty cartridges in the wheel of his gun.[11] Harrell later indicated that he shot four times, and the captain three times. During the shootout, Harrell only saw one suspect but believed there were more.[12] He thought the burglars shot at the light that Griswold was gripping in his hand at about heart level, and believed they were speaking Spanish.[13]

Detectives from the Wichita Police Department spent years trying to solve the murder of Griswold. As time went by, the citizens of Wichita became frustrated. Evidence of this could be seen in the local newspaper when *The Wichita Daily Eagle* published the following: "It is reported that police officers have information indicating the identity of Captain Griswold's murderers but that money is not available for use in locating them. Citizens were yesterday asking each other why the mayor does not find a way to secure money for someone to go and get these criminals."[14]

Detectives developed multiple suspects during the span of their investigation, and Governor Capper offered a reward for each of the suspected murderers' arrests and convictions on September 19, 1916.

The three men wanted at the time were brothers. It was believed that Ora, Frank, and Oscar Lee Lewis were responsible for the murders of Captain Griswold and William Sutton, a Wichita merchant. The same brothers were also wanted in St. Louis for the

---

10. "Wichita Police Captain Killed in Gun Battle," *The Wichita Eagle*, May 23, 1915.

11. "Captain Killed," *Wichita Eagle*.

12. "Burglars, Trapped in Store Slay Police Captain; Escape," *The Wichita Beacon*, May 24, 1915.

13. "Captain Killed," *Wichita Eagle*.

14. "Citizens Discuss Murders," *The Wichita Eagle*, October 19, 1915.

murder of two police officers.[15] However, they were never convicted of the murder of Griswold, nor was anyone else.

Another man, Frank Boaz, confessed to law enforcement in Kansas City that he killed Captain Griswold. Unfortunately, he later denied it and claimed he confessed to it to get drugs. According to Boaz, he was given "hop" after telling a made-up story of how the murder transpired.[16]

Griswold resided at 125 South Charles Avenue at the time of his death. He was survived by his wife and large family. Griswold served for several years with the Pueblo Police Department in Colorado before moving to Wichita.[17]

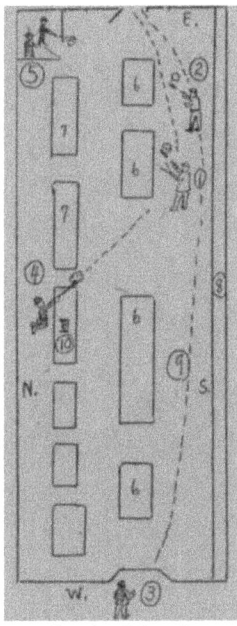

A Sketch of the Shooting at the A. E. Bump Shoe Store. The Wichita Beacon. May 24, 1915. Public Domain.

---

15. "Rewards for Wichita Slayers Exceed $3000," *The Topeka Daily Capital*, September 20, 1916.

16. "Confesses for Dope," *The Wichita Eagle*, October 23, 1921.

17. "Wichita Police Captain Killed in Gun Battle," *The Wichita Eagle*, May 23, 1915.

6

Detective William H. Ballard

Date: July 20, 1920
Day: Tuesday
Time: 2210 hours
Location: 151 North Wichita Street
Tour: Five years with the Wichita Police Department (1915-1920) - Four years as a deputy marshal of city court
Age: Fifty-two
Race: White
Gender: Male
Marital Status: Married
Military Veteran: Unknown
Children: Seven
Badge: Not applicable
Burial: White Chapel Memorial Gardens, Wichita, Sedgwick County, Kansas
Cause: Gunfire
Weapon: Gun - Harrington and Richardson .32 automatic
Offender Status: Convicted of first-degree murder
Offender Age: Twenty-four
Offender Race: White
Offender Gender: Male
Chief of Police at the Time: S. W. Zickefoose

Detective William H. Ballard. Wichita Police Department.

On Tuesday, July 20, 1920, at approximately 2210 hours, Detective William H. Ballard, a plain clothes detective, was shot and killed while searching a room, containing two occupants, for drugs and weapons. Officer Leroy "Jack" Weaver, a motor officer, and Detective Walter Rambo, also a plain clothes detective, were also wounded during the shooting.

The incident occurred inside a poorly maintained rooming house at 151 North Wichita Street, on the southwest corner of 1st Street and Wichita Street.[1] The three officers responded to a call made by Mrs. Frazier, who reported two individuals that went by "King" and "Berry" acting suspiciously in her residence.[2]

---

1. "Gunman Kills One and Wounds Two Policemen," *The Wichita Eagle*, July 21, 1920. Detective Walter Rambo was from Alva, Oklahoma, and served with the Woods County Sheriff's Office for eight years before moving to Wichita. He was elected Sheriff on two different occasions during his service for the county. At the time of the incident, Rambo had been with the Wichita Police Department for two years. He had a wife, son, and a daughter.

2. "Desperado Kills Officer Ballard and Wounds Two," *The Wichita Beacon*, July 21, 1920. About a month before the incident, Ballard and his family moved to 810 North Indiana Avenue. A burial plot was donated by the Old Mission Cemetery for the slain detective.

After Detective Rambo was treated at the hospital, he gave a statement to his fellow detectives that described how the events unfolded. The statement that he gave is as follows:

> We were called to 151 North Wichita to arrest some dope fiends. When we entered the room we found two men, said to be King and Berry, a dice box with some dice, and some dope. When I picked up the dice box I found a .32 automatic shell in the box. I then remarked "We had better look out, boys, there is an automatic here." I was bending over the bed, searching the mattress for dope, and Ballard was in the corner of the room searching some clothing that was hanging on the wall. Just as I remarked about the automatic, I heard a shot and also heard a man fall. As I raised up from looking under the mattress I was shot in the chin. This stunned me for a few minutes, but I heard two or three other shots fired. As I began to realize what was happening, I saw a man going out at the window, and grabbed him by the leg. As I grabbed him, some one hollowed [sic] "Get that big fellow," and I was struck over the head from behind. The men were both out of the window by this time, and had run off. I saw Ballard in the corner, and went to him. He was unconscious. I think Ballard was killed the first shot.[3]

Detective Ballard was shot with a .32 caliber revolver a total of three times, twice on the left side of his neck and once in the mouth. It was later discovered that the two bullets that struck Ballard's neck were lodged inside. Powder burns on his lips, broken teeth, and a cut tongue led investigators to believe he was shot in the mouth. Blood was streaming heavily from his mouth and left ear. A cut above his right eye may have been caused by the fall after being shot. Ballard's .38 caliber Smith and Wesson Special was holstered during the search.[4]

Rambo, who was lucky to have survived, was shot in his chin. The round struck very close to one of Rambo's jugular veins and exited approximately two inches from the entry point. The third officer at the scene, Weaver, had an entry wound to the bottom-side

---

3. "Gunman Kills One and Wounds Two Policemen," *The Wichita Eagle*, July 21, 1920.

4. "Gunman Kills One," *Wichita Eagle*.

of his jaw. The bullet subsequently traveled along his cheekbone, took out his left eye, and exited his forehead just above his eye.[5]

After realizing that the two suspects fled on foot, Rambo quickly made his way to a nearby telephone to inform others at police headquarters. After receiving the message, Desk Sergeant Rogers contacted Chief Zickefoose and informed him of the situation. An ambulance was called for Rambo and Weaver, who were taken to Wichita Hospital for treatment. After treatment, Rambo would give his statement at City Hall and then assisted in the search for the suspects.

Descriptions of the two suspects were sent out on the same night of the shooting. The early description of the first suspect was, "King, 22 to 25 years old. Five feet six. Hundred forty pounds. Black hair. Black eyes. Dark complexion. Dope fiend." The second suspect was described as, "_____24 years old. Five feet eleven. Hundred sixty-five pounds. Light complexion. Wearing khaki shirt. Good looking man." Chief Zickefoose gave orders to his officers to arrest the two suspects and to "take no chances. . . . Every known dope fiend in Wichita" was to be arrested.[6]

Weaver was able to remain conscious throughout the entire ordeal except during his operation at the hospital.[7] He would later tell others that he did not have his revolver during the search. He also believed he served in the same company, the 74th Sixth Regiment Marines, with one of the suspects.[8] Weaver remarked to family members and George Siefkin, an assistant city attorney, "I know who shot me; it was my buddy."[9]

Ed Frazier and his wife operated the rooming house where the incident took place. The dilapidated house consisted of eight rooms and a hallway. The Missouri Pacific train tracks ran in front of the residence. Mr. Frazier said the officers were inside the house for approximately five minutes when he heard the gunshots. After the shooting, Rambo used Frazier's phone to call for additional officers. Frazier indicated that he did not know much about the suspects, only that one of them was named "King."[10]

---

5. "Desperado Kills Officer Ballard and Wounds Two," *The Wichita Beacon*, July 21, 1920.

6. "Gunman Kills One and Wounds Two Policemen," *The Wichita Eagle*, July 21, 1920.

7. "Desperado," *Wichita Beacon*.

8. "Gunman Kills One," *Wichita Eagle*.

9. "Desperado," *Wichita Beacon*.

10. "Desperado," *Wichita Beacon*.

When called by a member of *The Wichita Beacon* and asked about the specific room the incident took place, Mrs. Frazier exclaimed, "It's the last one down the hall. I just got through scrubbing up the blood where that officer was killed. My, I hope I never have that experience again! It's terrible, I hope thay [sic] hang them dope fiends."[11]

Approximately two weeks before the murder, a man who went by the name of E. M. King rented a room at the Frazier house. E. M. King worked as a fireman for the Missouri Pacific, and he seemed like an honest person, according to Mrs. Frazier. He informed Mrs. Frazier that he had a "sickly" brother that might stop by, and to allow him to use his room if he desired. The pale, "sickly" brother showed up about five to six days later. Mrs. Frazier believed that the brother, "King," was up to mischief and was selling drugs.

Around 1900 hours on the night of the murder, "King" complained to Mrs. Frazier about his fireman brother taking all his clothes to the laundry. While displaying a blue-steeled revolver, the angry "King" made comments that he was going to kill his brother. Additional occupants of the rooming house saw "King" with guns on the same day. Mrs. Frazier stated that he went downtown on the night of the murder, and had returned just before 2200 hours, whistling as he entered the house. Another unknown man soon arrived and went to "King's" room. Mrs. Frazier had had enough of the drug-using brother, so she called the police to have the two males escorted from her house.[12]

The investigation eventually led to the suspects being apprehended and held in Kansas City. Harry Baird, who was twenty-four-years-old and probably the "sickly brother" that Mrs. Frazier referred to, was arrested on Saturday, July 24, 1920, in Independence, Missouri and taken to the jail in Kansas City. Charles "Chuck" Bledsoe, who was twenty-one at the time, was arrested in Kansas City on Thursday, August 5, 1920. Chief Zickefoose traveled to Kansas City after being informed that two prisoners there matched the description of Ballard's killers.[13]

Bledsoe would go on to indicate that he was a witness to the shooting and put the blame on who he called "Harry Barry," aka Harry Baird. At first, Baird denied to Chief Zickefoose that he was the killer of Ballard. After a two-hour interrogation, Baird confessed to the crime when he was confronted by statements made earlier by Bledsoe.

---

11. "Desperado Kills Officer Ballard and Wounds Two," *The Wichita Beacon*, July 21, 1920.

12. "Desperado," *Wichita Beacon*.

13. "Baird Confesses the Murder of Ballard," *The Wichita Beacon*, August 6, 1920.

He said the officers overlooked a revolver that was covered by his shirt. During the search of the room, Baird saw his chance to escape and used his weapon to do so. Baird remarked that he did not know why he did it.

The morning after the murder, it was discovered that a friend of Baird's aided his escape by taking him to Hutchinson. Detectives missed Baird by about four hours in Hutchinson. They continued to trail him to Atchison, Leavenworth, and then to Kansas City. The trail was lost when Baird was arrested in Independence, Missouri under the alias of "Walter Barry."

Charles Bledsoe was trailed to 12th Street and Baltimore Avenue in Kansas City on August 5, 1920. Captain Coffey would eventually receive a tip about Bledsoe's location at a specific time. He sent plain clothes officers to the location armed with a photo of Bledsoe.

Bledsoe appeared and was taken into custody without incident. He denied his identity at first but would later tell the truth after being shown a photo of himself by a detective.

During the interview, Bledsoe talked about the killing. He said one of the detectives who entered the room had made a comment that there was another pistol in the room because a tipster told them so. One of the other detectives replied that the second gun would not be located if it was indeed in the room. Bledsoe said the detective that made the original comment about the second gun reengaged his search of the room, and the other two officers turned their backs to Bledsoe and Baird. While they were not being monitored, Baird would fire multiple shots at the officers. He and Baird escaped the room, and he left Baird to go his own way.[14]

A signed statement by Baird perhaps provides the most consistent and understandable account of the unfolding, tragic event:

> I came to Wichita June 5, 1920, and spent two days here. I returned June 16 as Joe Palmyra. I obtained a room at 151 North Wichita Street with a Missouri Pacific fireman, Earl King. I met Bledsoe the first time I came to Wichita and he had been to the room two or three times. On the evening of July 20, both of us went to the room. About 10 p.m. Officers Ballard,

---

14. "Baird Confesses the Murder of Ballard," *The Wichita Beacon*, August 6, 1920. Officer Leroy Weaver's eye socket would go on to heal, and he eventually received an artificial eye.

Rambo and Weaver came. Weaver went to one window, Rambo the other, and Ballard went to the door and knocked. I asked who was there, and he said: "Jones." I asked again and he repeated. I said: "All right, wait a minute!" I was taking a shot and wanted to get my shirt on, as I thought they were officers and did not want them to see the scars on my arms. I opened the door and Ballard came in, then the others. Ballard said: 'What have you got on you?' I answered I had nothing, and he searched me. He took what little belongings I had and asked my name. I think I told him I was a fireman. He left me and started to search Bledsoe, and then searched the room and gathered up some things there. Weaver stood facing me, Ballard had his back turned, and Rambo stood sideways. I drew the gun which was under my shirt and which was overlooked by Ballard. Rambo had just made the statement: 'Boys, there ought to be a .32 automatic around her somewhere' and had started to renew the search of the house. He looked everywhere and then came back and they started to pick up the stuff they had found. When they started to pick it up, I pulled my gun and fired, shooting Rambo, then Ballard, then Weaver. As Ballard did not fall, I doubled back and shot him twice more. These officers had not said anything out of the way, neither had they done anything to cause such action. I do not know why I shot them. At the first shot, Bledsoe went thru the south window. Shortly after the shooting, I started to follow, but Rambo grabbed my legs. I was on the bed, hanging out the window with my face down. I turned over on my back and struck him over the head with my gun several times. The last blow must have knock him out as he turned loose and I got away. The gun I used was a Harrington and Richardson .32 automatic, now in the possession of Chief of Police Zickefoose. I went to Valley Center a short time later, and traded the gun for ten dollars' worth of dope. Then I returned to Wichita and went to Hutchinson on the Twenty-first, where I sold a Colt's automatic which I had hidden outside of the house at 151 North Wichita. It also is now in the possession of the chief. On the night of July 21, I went to Kansas City, and I was arrested there July 23. On July 24 I pleaded guilty to petit larceny received a six months' sentence and was from the county jail there until I was brought back to Wichita.[15]

Harry Baird was charged with the murder of Detective William H. Ballard, with the trial beginning in Judge Wall's court on Monday, November 15, 1920. County Attorney J. A. Conly and Deputy Tom Elcock were the prosecutors in the case, while Willard Glasco represented Baird.[16] To no one's surprise, a guilty verdict of first-degree murder was returned after only two hours of deliberation on Tuesday, November 16, 1920.[17] Baird was sentenced to life in prison and sent to Lansing Penitentiary. Many officers believed that Baird was one of the worst criminals that they had encountered in years.[18]

Charles Bledsoe was found "not guilty" for the murder of Detective Ballard on Thursday, February 17, 1921.[19] On Tuesday, April 19, 1921, Bledsoe was acquitted of the charge of assault with intent to kill a policeman on Officer Weaver. Weaver had testified at previous hearings that Bledsoe shot him. It is unclear if Weaver knew Bledsoe from his military days or if he was mistaken. Additional evidence of a military connection between Weaver and Bledsoe was never found.[20]

William H. Ballard and his large family lived at 1309 North Indiana Avenue for many years and moved from there about one month before his murder. He had spent five years with the police department and four years as a deputy marshal of city court. Originally from Indiana, Ballard moved to Butler County when he was eight years old. Before serving as a deputy marshal, he worked as a carpenter. Detective Ballard was survived by his wife, four sons, and three daughters.[21]

---

15. "Shot Rambo First and then Ballard," *The Wichita Beacon*, August 9, 1920.

16. "Jury is Chosen; Baird Hearing Set for Monday," *The Wichita Eagle*, November 13, 1920.

17. "Baird is Guilty in First Degree," *The Wichita Beacon*, November 16, 1920.

18. "Officers Think Baird Bad Actor," *The Wichita Beacon*, November 20, 1920.

19. "Charles Bledsoe Not Guilty," *The Sun*, February 18, 1921.

20. "Acquitted of Intent to Murder Policeman," *Springfield Republican*, April 20, 1921.

21. "Gunman Kills One and Wounds Two Policemen," *The Wichita Eagle*, July 21, 1920.

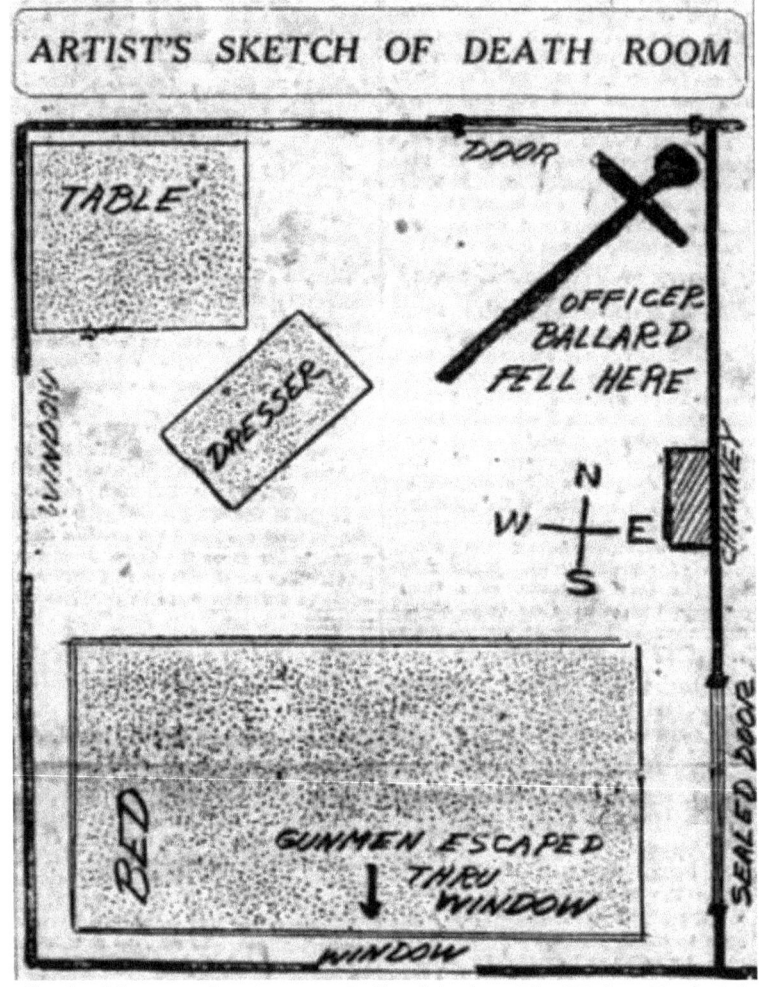

Sketch of the room that Detective Ballard died in. The Wichita Eagle. July 21, 1920. Public Domain.

7

PATROLMAN ALBERT L. YOUNG

Date: November 5, 1921
Day: Saturday
Time: 2045 hours
Location: Alley east of 11th Street and Lewellen Street
Tour: Over one year (1920 to 1921)
Age: Forty-four
Race: White
Gender: Male
Marital Status: Widow[1]
Military Veteran: Unknown
Children: Three
Badge: Not applicable
Burial: Englewood Cemetery, Englewood, Clark County, Kansas
Cause: Gunfire
Weapon: .38 caliber handgun
Offender Status: Unknown
Offender Age: Unknown
Offender Race: Unknown
Offender Gender: Unknown
Chief of Police at the Time: W. A. Scott

---

1. "Obituary," *The Meade County News*, June 1, 1911. Albert Young was married to Maggie Smith Young. She died on May 23, 1911, from ptomaine poisoning after eating ice cream. She was thirty years old. Albert and Maggie married on July 23, 1905, and they had three sons. The oldest son died at the age of six months, and the other two were four and two years old when their mother died.

Patrolman Albert L. Young. Wichita Police Department.

Patrolman Albert L. Young was shot to death by a man at 2045 hours on Saturday, November 5, 1921, near an alley between Lewellen Street and Jefferson Street, at 11th Street. Multiple people in the neighborhood indicated shots were exchanged between the patrolman and another person, with approximately nine shots being heard. Young's revolver was found to be empty when contact was made with him. It was not immediately known who shot Young, but a man in a white shirt was seen running south in the alley, and then west on 10th Street.[2]

C. M. Rathbone, who resided at 1134 North Jefferson Avenue, arrived quickly on the scene to find Young groaning slightly while on the ground with his head facing north.

---

2. "Wichita Policeman is Slain," *The Wichita Eagle*, November 6, 1921.

One of Young's sleeves were slightly on fire from one of his, or the assailant's, shots. A. Richardson, who lived at 1141 North Jefferson Avenue, reported hearing the shots at 2045 hours.

A boy named Richard Linden was delivering a package for the Riverside Pharmacy when he observed flashes from the revolvers and made his way toward the scene before realizing that a tragedy was unfolding. As he approached, he observed something in the street and used his flashlight to illuminate it. Realizing it was a human being on the ground, the boy began to yell for help, prompting several others to the scene.

George Young, a streetcar trainman, and Leon Young, a visitor of the city, were brothers of the patrolman and consulted with officers after his death. At the time of the shooting, the three brothers were living with Mrs. Cordell at 1125 North Lewellen Street.

Multiple theories arose after the shooting. One theory suggested a grudge existed between the suspect and Young. A second theory was that the suspect attempted to mug the patrolman, not realizing he was a law enforcement officer. The former theory, at first, was more heavily believed by those working on the case than the latter, although the cause of the grudge was not immediately known. Given that the suspect was wearing a white shirt at night, it was not conducive to the robbery theory.[3]

Pieces of information were revealed to law enforcement and the public over time, which caused peoples' beliefs to change and flip-flop between various theories. *The Wichita Eagle* reported the following, eight days after Young's murder:

> There are many theories as to the cause of the shooting but the man-hunters are working on the following theories.... That jealousy of a rival for the affections of some woman, was the cause and that the slayer either waylaid Young or met him at his home and walked down the alley with him.... That patrolman Young was mistaken for some other person who had an enemy and that the cause of the trouble was a woman.... That Young saw a hold-up or prowler in the alley and started after him.... That an attempt was made to hold him up.[4]

---

3. "Wichita Policeman is Slain," *The Wichita Eagle*, November 6, 1921.

4. "Seek the Woman," *The Wichita Eagle*, November 13, 1921.

R. T. McAuley, owner of the Riverside Pharmacy, believed the hold-up theory to be true because he observed two suspicious, intoxicated men inside his store around 2000 hours. The men purchased soda water and walked to the street. They were later seen, after the shooting, at the Potter grocery store, which was two blocks west of the pharmacy on 11th Street.[5]

Mrs. Cordell informed reporters with *The Eagle* that Young was never at home on Saturday, causing most people to believe he was on the way to his residence. Her interviews with law enforcement and the media were very brief due to her emotional state.

Albert's brother, Leon, informed police officers that he last saw Albert on Friday night around 2200 hours. Leon could not think of any reason why the incident transpired, or any person who had a problem with his brother. His other brother, George, also had no critical information for law enforcement.

A man named Wykoff Keach, who was in Riverside at the time of the shooting, heard seven shots. Shortly after that, he observed three men in a motor vehicle at the Riverside junction. One of the males quickly exited the vehicle and ran inside a filling station. A few minutes later, the male hurried back to the vehicle and left.

According to S. W. Zickefoose, Chief of Detectives at the time, no solid leads existed early in the case. However, some observations were made at the scene of the crime. A large tree near the start of the alley could have provided great cover for the suspect, and the upward angle of bullets recovered from a nearby structure suggests that the patrolman was on the ground when he fired some of the shots. As for Young's reputation, Zickefoose had only positive things to say about him.[6]

Young's law enforcement "brothers" said Young was one of the most well-liked officers in the Department, so their ability to narrow their focus on a specific suspect was not possible early-on in the investigation. The fact that Young was shot one time near the heart suggests that the shooter was an exceptional shot.[7]

The investigation revealed that Young exited a streetcar on Bitting Street sometime between 1900 hours and 2045 hours and walked east. Motorman Majors believed it was around 1900 hours at Bitting Street and 11th Street, along with six to eight other people.[8]

---

5. "Many Speculate about Shooting," *The Wichita Eagle*, November 7, 1921.

6. "Wichita Policeman is Slain," *The Wichita Eagle*, November 6, 1921.

7. "Seek the Woman," *The Wichita Eagle*, November 13, 1921.

8. "Speculate," *Wichita Eagle*.

Coroner D. G. Heckman believed the bullet was fired from a large caliber revolver and entered the breast about three inches left of Young's heart. $3.91 and a Y.M.C.A. membership card was in Young's pockets.[9] However, Zickefoose later said the bullet extracted from Young's body was a .38 caliber.[10]

Young spent most of his day on Saturday at the residence of Mrs. Zella Metcalf, at 403 Minnesota Avenue. A reporter for *The Wichita Eagle* was told by Mrs. Metcalf that Young left her residence around 1915 hours on Saturday evening. Before leaving, Young loaded his revolver while the five children of Mrs. Metcalf begged him to leave the gun at the residence so they could play with it. Young obviously declined, and while loading his revolver he said, "It is best to be prepared." Mrs. Metcalf told the reporter that Young's comment had no importance to the case, as it was said casually.

Mrs. Metcalf claims that Young would have told her if he was in fear of some other person. She said her husband, Earl Metcalf, was living in Dodge City with his parents at the time of the incident and denies Young's death was over her. She claimed her husband was friends with Young.[11] Mrs. Metcalf said Young was heading to his residence to obtain some tobacco before he was shot and killed by the assailant.[12]

Mattie Tapps, a cook who resided at 252 North Waco Avenue, told a reporter with *The Wichita Eagle* that approximately a week-and-a-half before the homicide, Young told her that he received letters threatening his life. Sometime during the last week of Young's life, it is believed that he burned the letters along with a large bundle of correspondence.[13]

No one was ever arrested or convicted of Young's murder. Many people believe Eddie Adams, a notorious gangster, or a member or his gang killed Young. About three months before the murder of Albert L. Young, Eddie Adams, Frank Foster, and George Weisgerber escaped from Lansing Penitentiary together.[14]

Six months before that, in February of 1921, Adams was on his way to the penitentiary in Jefferson City to serve a life sentence for murder when he escaped his guards and

---

9. "Wichita Policeman is Slain," *The Wichita Eagle*, November 6, 1921.

10. "Woman Says Slain Man Got Letters Threatening Him, *The Wichita Eagle*, November 8, 1921.

11. "Woman Talks of the Slain Man," *The Wichita Eagle,* November 7, 1921.

12. "Seek the Woman," *The Wichita Eagle*, November 13, 1921.

13. "Probe Report of Threatening Note," *The Wichita Eagle*, November 9, 1921.

14. "George Oldham Shot by Foster," *Winfield Daily Courier*, December 5, 1921.

slipped into the darkness. He robbed the Cullison State Bank in Pratt, Kansas a few days later and was arrested. Ignoring Missouri officials' pleas to extradite Adams to Missouri, Kansas officials kept him in the state, and he was tried, convicted, and sentenced to thirty years in Lansing for the robbery. After escaping from Lansing in August of 1921, he and his fellow criminals traveled to Wichita and became more organized and wreaked havoc throughout the region.

As Adams, Foster, Weisgerber, and Billy Fentelman were in the middle of a crime spree through Missouri and Iowa, they stopped on a country road near Murray, Iowa to get some rest after a bank robbery on October 19, 1921, about seventeen days before Young's murder.

At 1330 hours, Osceola County Sheriff E. J. West, a farmer named C. W. Jones, John Miller, Charley Eaton, and an unidentified posse member approached the killers' vehicle. Adams awoke and noticed the posse approaching, prompting him to warn his buddies and open fire on the group. Jones was killed, and Miller, Eaton, and the unidentified posse member were injured. The suspects stole the sheriff's car and made their way back to Kansas. They ditched the car, stole another vehicle, and continued their reign of terror.[15]

Patrolman Albert L. Young patrolled beat number five on Douglas Avenue, from Emporia to Main Street. He worked the night shift, from 2300 hours to 0700 hours. His two sons, Leonard and Arthur, ages twelve and eleven at the time of Young's death, lived with Young's parents in Englewood, Kansas.[16]

Seven years before the homicide, Young served as a fireman with the Santa Fe Railroad while living in Wellington, Kansas.[17] Two days after the death of Young, City Manager Earl G. Elliott announced that all police officers were required to partake in a regular pistol target practice, and the city would provide the ammunition.[18]

---

15. Bill Gagnon, "End of Gang Reign Cost 3 Lives Here," *The Wichita Eagle*, November 15, 1953.

16. "Wichita Policeman is Slain," *The Wichita Eagle*, November 6, 1921.

17. "Murdered Policeman Formerly Lived Here," *The Wellington Daily News*, November 9, 1921. Young's stay in Wellington, Kansas was short-lived, lasting only six months. He was briefly married to his second wife, Mary Benson, while living there. After Young moved back to Englewood, Kansas, Mary obtained a divorce from him on the grounds of desertion.

18. *The Coffeyville Daily Journal*, November 8, 1921.

8

PATROLMAN JAMES R. FITZPATRICK

Date: November 21, 1921
Day: Monday
Time: 0110 hours
Location: Harry Street and Hydraulic Avenue
Tour: Seven months (1921)
Age: Thirty
Race: White
Gender: Male
Marital Status: Married
Military Veteran: Yes - Army - World War I
Children: Two
Badge: Not applicable
Burial: Rochester Cemetery, Topeka, Shawnee County, Kansas
Cause: Gunfire
Weapon: .38 caliber handgun
Offender Status: Convicted of murder in Iowa
Offender Age: Twenty
Offender Race: White
Offender Gender: Male
Chief of Police at the Time: W. A. Scott

Patrolman James R. Fitzpatrick. Wichita Police Department.

Patrolman James R. Fitzpatrick, a motorcycle officer with the Wichita Police Department, was killed by a gunman who was in a vehicle on Friday, November 21, 1921, at 0110 hours. Fitzpatrick and Motorcycle Patrolman R. LaCroix were riding together on a motorcycle, with LaCroix driving and Fitzpatrick riding in the sidecar. Before the shooting, the two officers stopped a Buick automobile occupied by three men and three women at Harry Street and Hydraulic Avenue.

The occupants were subsequently informed they were under arrest, because the officers noticed the driver was acting strange, as if under the influence of alcohol or drugs. Fitzpatrick recognized the driver, George Macfarline, who had an arrest history for selling "habit forming" drugs. The occupants and the vehicle were not searched by the officers. The officers directed them to drive to police headquarters while the officers followed them.

The two vehicles traveled a short distance west on Harry Street when someone from inside the Buick fired shots, striking Fitzpatrick. Patrolman Fitzpatrick stood up in the sidecar and fell onto LaCroix, who did everything in his power to hang on to his comrade and control the motorcycle. Fitzpatrick died immediately. LaCroix was not able to return fire to the vehicle, which sped away west on Harry Street. He notified police headquarters, and every police officer and detective available responded. The investigation was conducted by S. W. Zickefoose, Chief of Detectives.[1]

A short time later, a farmer, George Oldham, was shot in his jaw at his home about six miles west of Winfield, Kansas, in Cowley County. It was believed the same suspects had engine trouble or ran out of fuel, and their car stopped in front of Oldham's farmhouse. They attempted to steal Oldham's vehicle when they shot him after he tried to intervene. Oldham survived the shooting.

Cowley County Sheriff Charles M. Goldsmith, Deputy Don Goldsmith, Chief of Police Fred Hoover (Winfield), and Officer Russell Kimberlain (Winfield) were called out around 0400 hours to search for the three men that shot Oldham. The officers came upon a Buick west of Winfield on the 48 School Road. A person hiding in the dark near the car fired on the approaching lawmen, who returned fire. The suspects were able to escape after they went to a nearby residence, the home of Wesley Orr, and stole his Chevrolet car. A couple of women's hats were in the suspects' Buick that broke down.[2]

Motorcycle Patrolman Ray Casner was later shot in the right thigh by an unknown male while watching a home associated with George Macfarline at 1229 South Washington Street at 1000 hours, the same day of Fitzpatrick's murder. It was Fitzpatrick's comment to LaCroix, just before his murder, that he recognized Macfarline in the vehicle that gave law enforcement their best lead, prompting Zickefoose to order a raid on the residence.

After the raid, Casner and Patrolman W. W. Wright were assigned to monitor the residence in hopes of locating Macfarline, who was wanted in Fitzpatrick's shooting. Nellie Miles, the wife of a well-known drug dealer, Clyde Miles, walked up to the residence with Tommie Youngman and were subsequently arrested by the officers and sent to police headquarters to be interviewed.[3] Mona Macfarline, George's wife, was arrested with P. D.

---

1. "3 Shot by Gunmen Today," *The Wichita Beacon*, November 21, 1921.

2. "Wichita Motor Cop Murdered Early Today," *Arkansas City Daily Traveler*, November 21, 1921.

3. "3 Shot," *Wichita Beacon*.

Orcutt when he escorted her home from the Fentelman's residence after watching their children.[4]

Patrolman's Ray Casner and W. W. Wright remained inside the residence, waiting for the suspects. Three men eventually arrived in a Dodge car. The driver remained in the vehicle while the other two started to enter the front of the house. As one of the men pushed the door open, Casner, holding a sawed-off shotgun, told the men to come inside. The men quickly realized the two were officers, prompting one suspect to run on foot while the other reached for a handgun in his pocket. Casner pointed the shotgun at the suspect and pulled the trigger, but there was no cartridge in the chamber. Casner threw the shotgun to the ground and went for his pistol, but the suspect was able to get a round off, which struck Casner's thigh.

The suspect fell off the porch and crawled next to the house for cover. Casner and Wright went to the back door to flank him, but the suspect ran to the Dodge and fled. Both officers fired their weapons at the suspects' vehicle as it drove away. Casner's wound was not life-threatening. He recognized Mr. Fentelman as the driver.

Coroner D. C. Heckman held an inquest for Fitzpatrick's death on the same day of the murder. A .38 caliber bullet entered the right side of Fitzpatrick's jaw and traveled to the left, according to *The Wichita Beacon*.

Immediately following Fitzpatrick's murder, known drug addict and notorious bank robber, Edward James "Eddie" Adams, was suspected by officers as being involved, along with another violent criminal named Frank Foster. Detectives also believed Adams and his gang may have been responsible for the death of Patrolman Young sixteen days earlier. They believed Adams, or illegal drugs, were in the vehicle, which is why the suspects did not want to drive to police headquarters after the vehicle stop. Adams and Foster were wanted men at the time for escaping Lansing Penitentiary. Robbery, safe-blowing, and holdups were some of the crimes that Adams and his gang were known for at the time.

The shooting of the farmer in Winfield was an indication to law enforcement that at least some of the suspects were traveling south toward Oklahoma. Carloads of Wichita police officers, along with officers from other agencies, were searching for the suspects in south Kansas and Oklahoma.

---

4. "Girls in Death Car Fear Killer of Fitzpatrick Will Slay Them," *The Wichita Beacon*, December 3, 1921.

During the morning of November 21, two cars containing multiple Wichita police officers exchanged gunfire with each other, believing the other vehicle was the gang. Damage was caused to both vehicles, and one officer lost a portion of his finger from a bullet.[5]

Not long after Patrolman Ray Casner's shooting, eighteen-year-old Wilma Fleming, and fifteen-year-old Annie Jones, were arrested by officers during a raid at Billy Fentelman's residence, at 1567 South Waco Avenue, and interviewed. Officers learned that Eddie Adams, Frank Foster, George Weisgerber, George Macfarline, Billy Fentelman, and P. D. Orcutt had a chicken dinner with Nellie Miles and several girls during the evening of November 20th. Afterwards, the group drove around in a couple of vehicles.

One of the vehicles was driven by Macfarline, with Nellie Miles and Adams sitting next to him in the front seat. The back seat contained Wilma Fleming, Annie Jones, and Frank Foster. Adams was armed with a .38-40 revolver, and Foster had a .38 Special when their vehicle was stopped by Fitzpatrick and LaCroix. The other vehicle, containing Fentelman, his wife, P. D. Orcutt, and a few others, drove off into the darkness when MacFarline's vehicle was stopped by the officers.

According to Fleming and Jones, it was Frank Foster who shot and killed Fitzpatrick after their vehicle was stopped by the officers. Immediately following the shooting, Foster turned his gun on Fleming and said, "We gotta bump these girls off here.... A fella can't depend on girls. They will squeal the minute the law gets them."[6] Adams pointed his gun at Foster's head and argued with him for being a coward for wanting to shoot the girls. The three women were dropped off at Fentelman's place and the three males drove to Cowley County.

George Macfarline, who was captured on a train in Augusta, Kansas not long after the Oldham shooting, claimed it was Foster who shot the farmer, George Oldham.[7] However, an article in *The Wichita Eagle* claimed it was Adams who shot Oldham, when Adams attempted to take Oldham's vehicle.[8] In early December of 1921, while Macfarline, Fleming, and Jones were sitting in jail, the three were so afraid of Foster, who

---

5. "3 Shot by Gunmen Today," *The Wichita Beacon*, November 21, 1921.

6. "George Oldham Shot by Foster," *Winfield Daily Courier*, December 5, 1921.

7. "Shot by Foster," *Winfield Daily Courier*.

8. Bill Gagnon, "End of Gang Reign Cost 3 Lives Here," *The Wichita Eagle*, November 15, 1953.

was still on the run, that they preferred to stay in jail for their safety.[9] Some sources claim Adams shot Patrolman Ray Casner, while other sources indicate it was Foster who shot him.

Patrolman James R. Fitzpatrick was hired by the Wichita Police Department on April 16, 1921. He was married and had two daughters, ages two and four years old. Friends told others that the family had very little personal property. Fitzpatrick attempted to obtain life insurance shortly before his death, but it was rejected due to a slight physical defect. He served as a captain in World War I. His last arrest occurred a few hours before he was killed. He arrested Nev Smith, of 1202 South Ida Street, for vagrancy and carrying a concealed weapon (a .45 caliber Colt).[10]

---

9. "George Oldham Shot by Foster," *Winfield Daily Courier*, December 5, 1921.

10. "3 Shot by Gunmen Today," *The Wichita Beacon*, November 21, 1921.

9

Detective Charles D. Hoffman

Date: November 25, 1921
Day: Incident occurred on Tuesday - Died on Friday
Time: Incident occurred at 1430 hours - Died at 0045 hours
Location: Incident occurred at 306 South Lawrence Avenue - Died at the hospital
Tour: Six years (with prior law enforcement experience) (1915-1921)
Age: Thirty-six
Race: White
Gender: Male
Marital Status: Married
Military Veteran: No
Children: Three
Badge: Not applicable
Burial: Old Mission Cemetery, Wichita, Sedgwick County, Kansas
Cause: Gunfire
Weapon: .38 Special
Offender Status: Shot and killed
Offender Age: Thirty-three or thirty-four
Offender Race: White
Offender Gender: Male
Chief of Police at the Time: W. A. Scott

Detective Charles D. Hoffman. Wichita Police Department.

On Tuesday, November 22, 1921, at 1430 hours, the two-day manhunt for the gangster, Eddie Adams, ended in a garage at 306 South Lawrence Avenue, but at a very high cost.

The business was called Driverless Motor Livery. According to Chief of Police W. A. Scott, an employee of a different local garage called him in the afternoon and indicated he believed one of the suspects in the recent shootings had just "asked for the hire of a car."[1] Detective Charles Hoffman, Detective Ed Bowman, and Detective D. C. Stuckey responded to the garage and learned that the suspect was refused a car and left east on Douglas Avenue with another male.

---

1. "Kill Adams and Rout Gang," *The Wichita Eagle*, November 23, 1921.

The detectives checked the area all the way to Washington Street with no luck, then decided to check the Driverless Motor Livery on South Lawrence Avenue after Stuckey brought it to their attention. When they arrived, they parked near the garage, according to Stuckey and Bowman.

The three detectives observed a man in the office, on the south end of the building, signing paperwork for a vehicle. By the time the detectives entered the building, Eddie Adams, the male seen signing the paperwork, was now standing and speaking with C. E. Jacks, the owner of the livery, about where he was residing. Hoffman walked close to Adams, sparking Adams to ask, "Your name is Hoffman, isn't it?" The detective told him he was, and he needed to see him. The two males took a couple of steps to the rear, according to Stuckey, while Adams exclaimed, "You'll have to come back here if you want to see me."[2] Adams made a subtle move, prompting Hoffman to grab him by the neck, and a struggle ensued.

Adams drew his gun, pressed it against Hoffman's abdomen, and fired twice. According to Bowman, Hoffman said, "My God, I'm shot." In a split second, Adams fired multiple times at Bowman at close range, striking him twice on his right side. Just after being shot, Bowman pointed his semi-automatic at Adams' head and fired, causing Adams to fall backward to the ground. As Hoffman was lying on the cement floor to the north, Bowman stood over the dying Adams, who raised his gun in a final effort, and fired a round, grazing Bowman's nose and powder-burning his face.[3]

As Adams and Bowman were focused on each other, Stuckey moved over to a nearby post and used it to steady his aim. He fired three times, and Adams was dead after the final shot. The entire physical altercation occurred within a matter of seconds.[4] One round appeared to have entered Adams' right cheek and exited behind the right side of his jaw.[5]

---

2. "Kill Adams and Rout Gang," *The Wichita Eagle*, November 23, 1921.

3. "Kill Adams," *Wichita Eagle*.

4. "Hoffman Did Not Recognize Adams, Stuckey Believes," *The Wichita Beacon*, November 22, 1921.

5. "Kill Adams," *Wichita Eagle*.

Both Detective D. C. Stuckey and Detective Ed Bowman later received equal credit for the killing of Adams by the coroner's jury during an inquest on Tuesday, November 29, 1921.[6]

Hoffman died on Friday, three days after the gunfight, at the hospital at 0045 hours. Dr. W. P. Callahan said the immediate cause of his death was general peritonitis, which set in two hours before his death. One of the soft-nosed .38 Special bullets entered the left side of Hoffman's abdomen, severed the colon and lodged in his spine, causing paralysis.[7]

The investigation revealed that J. C. Burns, who lived at 310 South Lawrence Avenue, introduced Eddie Adams to the manager of the livery where the incident occurred, and that Foster and Adams used the Burns residence as a hideout. Police searched the residence and located money, guns, ammunition, tools, and other items used and taken by the gang during their various robberies and burglaries. Burns and his wife, who had no criminal records, were charged with being accessories to the crimes.

While the roundup of criminals at the time resulted in several people being booked into the local jail, Frank Foster and George Weisgerber remained on the run.

Weisgerber was eventually arrested by the police. Zickefoose learned that Foster and two others stole E. H. Eager's vehicle and left for St. Joseph, Missouri. Zickefoose notified the authorities there, who spotted the empty stolen vehicle and conducted surveillance on it.

Foster was apprehended on December 19, 1921, when he and five others started to get in the vehicle. Foster, his brother-in-law, Robert Maddox, and Marion Cook were extradited back to Wichita for trial. Authorities from Iowa traveled to Wichita and begged for the extradition of Weisgerber, Fentelman, and Foster for the murder of C. W. Jones. Kansas authorities eventually agreed to extradite the three criminals on the belief they would be tried and executed for the murder, because Iowa had capital punishment at the time while Kansas did not.

Foster, Weisgerber, and Fentelman were convicted of murder on March 7, 1921, in Osceola District Court, after Foster confessed in court. Surprisingly, Judge Homer R. Fuller sentenced the three to life in prison at Fort Madison, angering many Kansas

---

6. "Detectives Get Equal Credit for Killing Adams," *The Wichita Beacon*, November 30, 1921.

7. "Charles Hoffman, Detective, Dies; Adams' Last Victim," *The Wichita Beacon*, November 25, 1921.

authorities. However, there were no parole boards at the time in Iowa, so the odds of them ever being released were believed to be slim.[8]

According to officers, Hoffman often expressed his aversion to taking another human's life, and that he always takes his prisoners alive. "Therefore, it is pointed out, his death... would be nothing more or less than martyrdom to a principle."[9] In this case, Hoffman lived up to his belief and was a hero, but he made the ultimate sacrifice for it.

The night after Eddie Adams was killed, the police held seventeen men and twenty women at the jail for questioning. Not long after the shootout, forty-one people were arrested, solving various crimes in five states. While not every crime committed by the Eddie Adams Gang was solved, the gang was broken, and life in the city eventually returned to normal.

Local cemetery owners at the time did not want the body of Eddie Adams buried on their land. After being displayed publicly at the City Undertaking Co., his body was transported to the University of Kansas Medical Center. Due to a fire in 1943 that destroyed records at the medical center, along with incomplete mortuary records, the location of Eddie Adams' remains are unknown.[10]

Chief W. A. Scott described Detective Charles D. Hoffman as the best detective in the Department, as well as a friend.

Hoffman resided with his wife, his ten-year-old son, and his two daughters, age nine and four, at 1232 North Jackson Avenue. He grew up in Wellington and Caldwell, where his father was the night marshal. About fifteen years before his death, Hoffman was appointed city marshal of Caldwell.[11]

---

8. Bill Gagnon, "End of Gang Reign Cost 3 Lives Here," *The Wichita Eagle*, November 15, 1953.

9. "Kill Adams and Rout Gang," *The Wichita Eagle*, November 23, 1921.

10. Beccy Tanner, "Notorious Bandit Holds Colorful Spot in History," *The Wichita Eagle*, July 15, 1993.

11. "Charles Hoffman, Detective, Dies; Adams' Last Victim," *The Wichita Beacon*, November 25, 1921.

10

Detective Charles E. Galloway

Date: July 15, 1923
Day: Incident occurred on Sunday - Died on a different Sunday
Time: Incident occurred during morning hours - Died at 1225 hours
Location: Incident occurred at Douglas Avenue and Cleveland Avenue - Died at Saint Francis Hospital
Tour: Eight years (1912-1923) (a break in service for about three years)
Age: Thirty-nine
Race: White
Gender: Male
Marital Status: Married
Military Veteran: Unknown
Children: One
Badge: Not applicable
Burial: Maple Grove Cemetery, Wichita, Sedgwick County, Kansas
Cause: Duty-related illness
Weapon: Not applicable
Offender Status: Not applicable
Offender Age: Not applicable
Offender Race: Not applicable
Offender Gender: Not applicable
Chief of Police at the Time: W. A. Scott

Detective Charles E. Galloway. Wichita Police Department.

Charles E. Galloway, who went by "Charlie," eventually suffered from blood poisoning because of a laceration to one of his toes while removing victims from a danger zone during flooding. He began feeling ill around Wednesday, June 20, 1923, and went to Saint Francis Hospital at the end of June. Galloway later died on Sunday, July 15, 1923. He joined the Department in 1912 and had a break in service for approximately three years.[1]

During the morning hours on Sunday, June 10, 1923, Galloway and other officers were rescuing victims around Douglas Avenue and Cleveland Avenue where there was heavy flooding. He fell into an open manhole, causing a cut and bruising to his left foot. His condition slowly grew worse over time, leading to acute renal failure.[2]

---

1. "Galloway Seriously Ill," *The Wichita Eagle*, July 11, 1923.

2. "Blood Poisoning Fatal to Charles Galloway Today," *The Wichita Eagle*, July 15, 1923.

The Wichita Eagle described Galloway as the "worst enemy of bootleggers, bad women, and law violators of every kind in Wichita."[3] He was zealous and sometimes radical in his pursuit of criminals and presented a rough and gruff personality on the outside. However, he treated young men, young women, and those who deserved a second chance with kindness, in hopes of altering their downhill path towards a positive one. While some bootleggers may have rejoiced at the passing of this determined enforcer, the large majority of those that he arrested had respect for him.

About a month prior to Galloway's death, he arrested a male who was about twenty years old for writing a bad check. The day before Galloway died, the male showed up at the police station and left eight dollars for Galloway. It was the last weekly installment that he owed the detective, who loaned the male, with no previous criminal record, the money to make good on the check that he wrote.

A few weeks before Galloway's death, he arrested a mother of five children on a charge of "lewdly abiding." He spoke with her at the police station and learned about her life difficulties. Later, he convinced the court to give her a reduced fine, which he paid and allowed her to pay him back whenever she could afford to. Her first payment was mailed to the station the day before Galloway died.

George Siefkin, the assistant city attorney, indicated that he had one regret: "I wish Charlie had lived a year or two longer to see the realization of that to which he had dedicated his life – the extermination of the liquor traffic in Wichita. It is gone practically now; it's not as bad as it was even two years ago, and it is all due to the untiring efforts of Charlie Galloway."[4]

Galloway was born on May 1, 1884, in Prescott, Arkansas. Before coming to Wichita, he was a preacher for the Methodist Episcopal Church. Ultimately, he came to Wichita to make more money to support his family.[5] He was survived by his wife, Bessie Galloway, and his five-year-old son, Charles Franklin Galloway.

---

3. "Law and Order has Lost One of Its Best Friends," *The Wichita Eagle*, July 16, 1923.

4. "Law and Order," *Wichita Eagle*.

5. "Law and Order," *Wichita Eagle*.

11

PATROLMAN ROBERT C. SCUDDER

Date: November 30, 1923 (The day after Thanksgiving)
Day: Incident occurred on Wednesday - Died on Friday
Time: Incident occurred at 2330 hours - Died at 1245 hours
Location: Incident occurred at 414 ½ East Douglas Avenue - Died at Wichita Hospital
Tour: Two years, three months (1921-1923)
Age: Thirty-seven
Race: White
Gender: Male
Marital Status: Yes
Military Veteran: Yes - Kansas National Guard
Children: Three
Badge: Not applicable
Burial: Old Mission Cemetery, Wichita, Sedgwick County, Kansas
Cause: Gunfire
Weapon: .32 automatic handgun[1]
Offender Status: Convicted of fourth-degree manslaughter
Offender Age: Twenty-three
Offender Race: White
Offender Gender: Male
Chief of Police at the Time: W. A. Scott

---

1. "Foor's Victim Dies," *The Emporia Gazette*, November 30, 1923.

Patrolman Robert C. Scudder. The Wichita Eagle. December 1, 1923. Public Domain.

Patrolman Robert C. Scudder was shot by Raymond H. Foor of Covington, Kentucky, on Wednesday, November 28, 1923, at 2330 hours, after Foor was ejected from a dance hall at 414 ½ East Douglas Avenue. Despite being shot, Scudder chased the suspect down the stairs, who then ran west along Douglas Avenue. As Scudder pursued Foor, he fired multiple shots at him, which missed Foor, and one round struck Perry Hall, a citizen, in the right leg.[2] Scudder died at Wichita Hospital two days later.

After the shooting, Foor fled Wichita. Law enforcement eventually caught up to him while he was on the Santa Fe No. 8 train in Emporia, Kansas on Thursday morning. Foor fired his handgun at police officers after they boarded the train and, in response, he was shot by Lyon County Undersheriff John Austin. After Scudder died in Wichita, an inquest was set for the following Wednesday.[3]

Mrs. Scudder said she was in "constant apprehension" because of her husband's job, especially when he was stationed at 18th Street and Lawrence Avenue (Broadway Avenue today). Back then, 18th Street and Lawrence Avenue must have felt relatively

---

2. "Wichita Policeman Near Death," *The Wichita Eagle*, November 29, 1923.

3. "Scudder Death Inquest is Set for Wednesday," *The Wichita Eagle*, December 2, 1923.

far away from the center of Wichita. He transferred downtown for a few days to relieve Officer Lyle, which made Mrs. Scudder feel better because her husband was closer.

Scudder had kissed his family goodnight, as usual, before he went to work on the night he was shot.[4] Later on, Scudder's family was awakened and informed that he was shot. On Thursday evening, he became conscious enough to recognize his children and Patrolman Dan Carrier, a coworker. He died on Friday, November 30, 1923, at 1245 hours in the hospital.[5]

Funeral services for Scudder occurred the following Monday at Grace Presbyterian Church. He was buried at Old Mission Cemetery.[6]

A warrant for first-degree murder was issued for Foor while he was in the hospital on the same day Scudder was buried.[7]

Foor was a time-lock expert employed by the Mosler Lock Company. Before the incident, he was in Wichita examining time locks on the vaults at the Fourth National Bank during the afternoon.[8] Details about Scudder's killing came out during the inquest.

The coroner's jury consisted of George Stirling, W. S. Warner, H. F. Hancock, W. Peters, J. H. Somers, and C. E. Jeys. The jury concluded that Scudder died from "the effects of gun shot wounds, the gun being in the hands of Ray H. Foor."[9] This finding made it possible to hold Foor on a charge of first-degree murder.

The Wichita Eagle indicated the part of the inquest that captured the most attention occurred during Violet Patterson's testimony. Violet was the female that Foor was dancing with before he shot Scudder. According to the newspaper, she tried to "justify Foor's action in brandishing a pistol when he was censured by the management of the dance hall for dancing indecently. Miss Patterson's testimony indicated that she was highly indignant because Foor's conduct had been questioned."[10] She denied talking to Foor since the shooting. However, she later told employees of newspapers that Foor's

---

4. "Believed Her Husband Would be Safe on Down-town Beat," *The Wichita Eagle*, December 1, 1923.

5. "Thank Others for Helping Capture Scudder's Slayer," *The Wichita Eagle*, December 1, 1923.

6. "Robert Scudder Buried Monday," *The Wichita Eagle*, December 4, 1923.

7. "Arraign Foor as Soon as He Can Leave Hospital," *The Wichita Eagle*, December 4, 1923.

8. "Admits the Shooting of Wichita Policeman but Reason Unknown," *The Wichita Eagle*, November 30, 1923.

9. "Foor Fired Shot Killing Scudder is Jury's Report," *The Wichita Eagle*, December 6, 1923.

10. "Foor Fired Shot," *Wichita Eagle*.

brother was in town talking with witnesses, and that she had spoken with him. She also told them, and law enforcement, that she did not know Foor's name and only danced with him one time.

The doorkeeper to the dance hall was H. C. Harrison. He said he warned Foor about his dancing behavior, as multiple people had complained to management. Foor pointed a pistol at him and said that there "are not enough of you [***] up here to put me out of this hall."[11] He also made threats to kill Harrison. A short time later, shots were heard downstairs where Foor and Scudder encountered each other.

R. S. DeHay, who lived at 511 ½ East Douglas Avenue, went with Scudder up some stairs after he arrived. The man who called for the police, W. C. Wiggers, pointed Foor out to Scudder as being the suspect who pulled out the gun during the disturbance with management. According to DeHay, Scudder contacted Foor and asked him where he was going. Foor indicated he was going home. As Scudder reached toward Foor and said, "Give me your gun," Foor started shooting at Scudder while DeHay was nearby.[12]

The Novelty Theater's motion picture operator, C. W. Grey, testified that he called for an ambulance after Scudder was shot, which took him to Wichita Hospital. Chief of Detectives S. W. Zickefoose, Clerk of the City Court C. O. Hancock, Superintendent of Public Welfare Dr. Dewey H. Cooper, and R. A. Brown also testified during the inquest.[13]

Not long after the shooting, law enforcement learned Foor was registered at the Hotel Broadview, where he quickly checked out after the incident and tried to cash a check but was denied by an employee of the hotel. He paid his fare for a ride to Hutchinson on the Arkansas Valley Interurban Railway, but he changed cars at the Van Arsdale to go to Newton.[14]

After arriving in Newton, Foor took a taxi to the Santa Fe depot and boarded a train to go eastbound, where he got off at Florence. Meanwhile, word was spreading from town to town about Foor's involvement, and it was suspected that he was on the Santa Fe

---

11. "Foor Fired Shot Killing Scudder is Jury's Report," *The Wichita Eagle*, December 6, 1923.

12. "Foor Fired Shot," *Wichita Eagle*.

13. "Foor Fired Shot," *Wichita Eagle*.

14. "Admits the Shooting of Wichita Policeman but Reason Unknown," *The Wichita Eagle*, November 30, 1923.

passenger train. At Florence, he bought a ticket for Kansas City. The nervous Foor held a handgun in his lap when officers caught up to him in Emporia.[15]

Much of the credit for capturing Foor was given to Bob Pryor and H. S. Hensley, plain clothes officers, and Sergeant "Kid" Yeager, who tracked his path to Newton and notified other agencies. Also assisting was the Sheriff of Harvey County, Carl E. Adams, the Chief Santa Fe Operator in Newton, John Utterbach, the Chief Special Agent in Newton, C. E. Atwell, and Florence Police Chief Ike Ikenbarger. The cooperation between the various men and agencies allowed authorities in Emporia to be notified in a timely manner and respond to the information.[16]

Lyon County Undersheriff John Austin later brought Foor's gun to the inquest and testified that Foor fired at Emporia police officers when they went to capture him. As previously indicated, Austin shot Foor in response.

Ray Foor was close to death in Memorial Hospital in Emporia during the night of Thursday, November 29, 1923, when he asked, "How is that policeman I shot in Wichita?" After being told by a hospital attendant that the officer had died (which was not accurate at that time), Foor replied, "Well, he has nothing on me; we're going the same route." This was the first known admission by Foor that he was the person who shot Scudder. When asked why he shot the officer, Foor said, "I know I can not live and I'm not saying anything."[17]

An armed guard remained near Foor because he threatened multiple times to take his own life. Foor later told Chief Zickefoose that he shot Scudder because he did not want to be arrested. When asked why he did not want to be arrested, Foor said he did not want to talk anymore. However, he did say, "I might as well be dead as having the penitentiary staring me in the face."[18]

As Foor recovered in the hospital and some time passed, he gave additional details of the incident. He was quoted as saying, "I was leaving the dance hall because the management objected to my way of dancing. . . . and when I reached the top of the stairway I saw the policeman coming up. I tried to give the pistol to a man behind me, but he wouldn't take it. In my attempt to hide it, it was discharged, the bullet hitting the

---

15. "Admits the Shooting of Wichita Policeman but Reason Unknown," *The Wichita Eagle*, November 30, 1923.

16. "Thank Others for Helping Capture Scudder's Slayer," *The Wichita Eagle*, December 1, 1923.

17. "Admits the Shooting," *Wichita Eagle*.

18. "Guard is Placed at Bedside of Man who Murdered Scudder," *The Wichita Eagle*, December 1, 1923.

patrolman. I did not want to be arrested with the gun, and I did not intentionally shoot the officer."[19]

Foor recovered enough to stand trial in June of 1924. The trial was held in Judge Jesse D. Wall's division of the district court. The prosecutor's case consisted of sixteen witnesses, five exhibits, Scudder's bullet-ridden uniform, Foor's gun, and two magazines with cartridges.

The first witness was Dr. D. H. Cooper, a city physician, who testified the bullet entered just above and to the right of Scudder's navel. The bullet stopped just under the skin in his back.

R. S. DeHay gave a more detailed description of Scudder and Foor's conversation when they contacted each other on the stairs:

> Scudder said, "Where you going?" and Foor replied, "I'm going home." Scudder then asked, "what have you been doing up there?" and Foor replied, "I haven't been doing anything." Scudder then asked, "what do you got there?" reaching out and grabbing Foor by the throat or chin and pushing his chin back. "Give me that gun," he said, but just as he grabbed Foor's chin Foor brought his gun up from his side and fired.[20]

Katherine Scudder took the stand while holding her baby and identified her dead husband's uniform and police cap. She did not have any further testimony.

Two special officers that worked for the Santa Fe railroad testified that after Foor was shot, he said, "You think you're a good shot, Jack, but you never did this." Foor had two bullet holes in his chest, and officers claimed that only one shot came from an officer. The officers' testimony cleared up confusion about the two wounds, that one of the wounds was caused by an accidental discharge by Foor after he was shot and fell to the floor.[21]

---

19. "Accidentally Shot Scudder Foor Asserts," *The Wichita Eagle*, December 3, 1923.

20. "Foor Shot Self During Gun Fight, Officers Testify," *The Wichita Eagle*, June 27, 1924.

21. "Foor Shot Self," *Wichita Eagle*.

Ray Foor's defense was that he took two capsules of what he thought was headache powder that he received from an unknown male. The powder, the defense claimed, was cocaine, and caused Foor to be in an altered state of mind when he shot Scudder.[22]

Four doctors were called to the stand during the trial to discuss the effects of cocaine on the body. Their testimonies varied widely. Foor's attorney claimed that Foor was not responsible for Scudder's death because he was unknowingly under the influence of cocaine and was unaware of his actions. The prosecution disagreed and argued that cocaine would have stimulated Foor's mind and body, causing him to be aware of his actions.[23] Sadly, the defense attorneys were successful and Foor was convicted of fourth-degree manslaughter.

Foor served one year and eight months in Lansing Penitentiary for killing Robert Scudder. *The Wichita Eagle* published a photo of Averill Gay, a female from Wichita who traveled to Kansas City when Foor was released to marry him. Their romance developed while Foor was in the Sedgwick County jail, awaiting trial.[24]

Patrolman Robert C. Scudder joined the Wichita Police Department on August 21, 1921. He served eighteen years with the National Guard and was promoted to the rank of captain. He was a Mason, belonged to the Knights of Pythias, and was a member of the Baraca Men's Bible School at the First Baptist Church.[25]

---

22. "Hold Ray H. Foor Responsible for Scudder's Death," *The Wichita Eagle*, July 2, 1924.

23. "Foor's Case Goes to Jury Today," *The Emporia Gazette*, June 30, 1924.

24. "Miss Averill Gay," *The Wichita Eagle*, March 15, 1926.

25. "Thank Others for Helping Capture Scudder's Slayer," *The Wichita Eagle*, December 1, 1923.

12

Patrolman Harrison R. Brown

Date: January 5, 1925
Day: Incident occurred on Sunday - Died on Monday
Time: Incident occurred at 1810 hours - Died at 1530 hours
Location: 13th Street and Wabash Avenue
Tour: Three years (1922-1925)
Age: Forty-one
Race: Black
Gender: Male
Marital Status: Married
Military Veteran: Unknown
Children: None
Badge: Not applicable
Burial: Shawnee Cemetery, Shawnee, Johnson County, Kansas
Cause: Gunfire
Weapon: .32 caliber revolver
Offender Status: Plead guilty to second-degree murder
Offender Age: Twenty-four
Offender Race: Black
Offender Gender: Male
Chief of Police at the Time: T. J. Thompson

Patrolman Harrison R. Brown. Wichita Police Department.

Patrolman Harrison R. Brown was shot below the heart by a black male, later identified as Douglas "Duke" Kelley, in the Makin Eye Drug Store at 13th Street and Wabash Avenue on Sunday, January 4, 1925, at 1810 hours. The bullet traveled through his spleen. Brown's wife gave more than a pint of blood during a blood transfusion in an attempt to save his life.[1]

Neighborhood residents identified Douglas Kelley as the suspect who shot Brown and fled. Police believed Brown followed Kelley on foot after Brown was told that Kelley was carrying a gun. According to two witnesses, Homer Turner, of 1326 North Indiana Avenue, and A. P. Halbrook, of 1145 North Ohio Avenue, Brown had entered the drug store to call headquarters after he lost track of Kelley, only to see him standing a few feet inside the business. After Brown asked to speak with him, Kelley drew a revolver

---

1. "Negro Policeman Shot Here Sunday May Not Recover," *The Wichita Eagle*, January 5, 1925.

from under his overcoat and fired. Kelley fled out of the store and up the street as Brown emptied his revolver. Brown fell in the arms of Homer Turner, who tried to help the officer.

The gun Kelley used was a .32 caliber revolver, and the bullet entered Brown's left side and traveled in an upward motion towards his heart. The bullet was not extracted.

Some citizens told police that they believed Kelley got into a Buick car and headed in the direction of Newton. Captain J. G. Yeager led the search for Kelley with several officers.

Deputy Roy Criswell told the public that Kelley's residence had been raided multiple times before in attempts to find illegally owned substances, but no liquor was located. Kelley did not have a known criminal record. He was 6'3" and weighed approximately 189 pounds, wearing overalls, a black overcoat, a black cap, and brown shoes. He had a wife at the time. Kelley was unknown to the two witnesses, but they believed they could identify him.[2]

Brown died at Saint Francis Hospital on Monday, January 5, 1925, at 1530 hours, about an hour and fifteen minutes after he identified Douglas Kelley as the man who shot him.

A veteran Winfield police officer, George Nicholas, arrested Kelley after the Santa Fe No. 11 train pulled into the city. After being transported to Wichita, Kelley gave Robert L. Pryor, Chief of Detectives, a full confession.

> "Yes, I shot him. He entered the drug store and yelled for me to put up my hands. I did not know he was an officer, so I grabbed my gun and fired as I turned. When I saw what I had done, I was scared and ran. I walked to Mulvane, and from there bought a ticket to Guthrie, Okla."[3]

Patrolman Brown gave his statement, between gasps for breath, to Harry C. Castor, deputy county attorney, and Frank Crow, deputy city court marshal, before he died. He indicated he never met Kelley before the shooting and did not know his motive. Multiple residents gave sworn statements to police indicating they heard Kelley make threats to kill Brown the next time he saw him. Some residents believed Mrs. Brown was formerly

---

2. "Negro Policeman Shot Here Sunday May Not Recover," *The Wichita Eagle*, January 5, 1925.

3. "Patrolman Dies After Assailant Admits Shooting," *The Wichita Eagle*, January 6, 1925.

married to Kelley before she married the patrolman, but Kelley said he never met her before.

Kelley claimed he shot one time at Brown with his small caliber revolver, but as Brown returned fire, Kelley shot back twice with a larger gun. Both of his firearms were seized when Kelley was arrested in Winfield. Kelley denied drinking alcohol around the time of the incident.[4]

During Kelley's arraignment in Judge Jesse D. Wall's courtroom on Tuesday, January 7, 1925, the defendant wanted to plead guilty to first-degree murder. However, he said he did not mean to kill Brown. The judge had to explain to him that a guilty plea for first-degree murder would result in a sentence of life in prison, and he assigned James Conly to defend him. Conly explained to Kelley that the guilty plea would mean he premeditated the murder. Thus, Kelley entered a not guilty plea, and the trial was set for January 12, 1925. Kelley waived his preliminary hearing in Judge Fred K. Hammer's courtroom earlier in the day. His bond was set at $10,000.

Kelley was a farmer from Oklahoma who came to Wichita a little over a year before the murder. He worked for the Dold Packing Company and had three sisters and one brother living in Wichita at the time. He told police during his confession that one of his sisters, Charlotte Taylor, was married on the Saturday before the shooting and he left his firearm at her residence at 1745 North Ohio Avenue. When he encountered Brown, he was in the process of returning it to his home at 1603 North Ohio Avenue, where he lived with his other sisters and brother.

Patrolman Harrison R. Brown's funeral services were held the Thursday after he was murdered at Saint Paul's A. M. E. Church at 1756 North Piatt Avenue. His body was sent to Shawnee Cemetery in Shawnee, Johnson County, Kansas for burial.[5] Brown was married three months before his death. He worked on the 13th Street and Wabash Avenue beat since October of 1924, which was created by the City Commission after they received numerous petitions from citizens who were complaining of crime in that area. Before that, Brown walked the North Main Street beat.[6]

Brown was known to greet everyone with a smile. According to *The Negro Star*, he was "very conservative in his dealing with men and was thought to be one of the best

---

4. "Patrolman Dies After Assailant Admits Shooting," *The Wichita Eagle*, January 6, 1925.

5. "Slayer Changes Plea, Deciding to Stand Trial," *The Wichita Eagle*, January 7, 1925.

6. "Negro Policeman Shot Here Sunday May Not Recover," *The Wichita Eagle*, January 5, 1925.

policemen in the city. We are not able to figure out why a person would want to kill the officer of the law, when they are given for the protection of all."[7]

The deputy county attorney, Harry Castor, went to Wellston, Oklahoma and obtained depositions from multiple people regarding the reputation and character of Douglas Kelley. On Monday, March 9, 1925, Kelley plead guilty to second-degree murder in Judge Grover Pierpont's courtroom. He was sentenced to forty years in prison.[8]

---

7. "Policeman Brown Killed," *The Negro Star*, January 9, 1925. *The Negro Star* was a newspaper created by Hollie T. Sims in Greenwood, Mississippi in 1908. Due to racial challenges, he moved the newspaper to Wichita, Kansas in 1919. The company provided the black community with news and updates until production ceased in 1953.

8. "Kelley Gets 40 Years," *The Wichita Eagle*, March 10, 1925.

13

Detective Edward W. Hall

Date: April 10, 1925
Day: Friday
Time: 0115 hours
Location: 1100 North Hillside Avenue
Tour: Two years (1923-1925)
Age: Twenty-eight
Race: White
Gender: Male
Marital Status: Married
Military Veteran: Yes
Children: None
Badge: Not applicable
Burial: Hoisington Cemetery, Hoisington, Barton County, Kansas
Cause: Gunfire
Weapon: .38 Special
Offender Status: Never convicted
Offender Age: Unknown
Offender Race: Unknown
Offender Gender: Unknown
Chief of Police at the Time: T. J. Thompson

Detective Edward W. Hall. Wichita Police Department.

The murder of Detective Edward W. Hall is an unsolved mystery. He was shot and killed on North Hillside Avenue near the entrance of Highland Cemetery on Friday, April 10, 1925, at approximately 0115 hours. He was with his partner, Detective Dick Burnside, at the time of his death. There were multiple different theories on how Hall was murdered, but none of them resulted in a conviction or gave closure to the public majority.

Hall was from Hoisington, Kansas where he worked for the Missouri Pacific Railroad before coming to Wichita several years before his murder. After arriving in Wichita, he worked for multiple electrical firms before joining the Wichita Police Department. Sources vary regarding his length of service in the Department, ranging from two to three years. He and his wife resided at 1725 South Market Street at the time of his death. Hall belonged to the Midian Temple of the Shrine, a masonic group.[1]

Shortly after the murder, Detective Burnside indicated that he and Detective Hall approached two men who were at the filling station of the Standard Oil Company, at 13th Street and Hillside Avenue. As the officers approached them, the pair ran to a Ford

---

1. "Sealed Verdict is Returned in Ed Smith Trial," *The Wichita Eagle*, March 11, 1927.

automobile and drove away. The detectives caught up with the suspects and stopped them. Detective Hall asked why their headlights were not burning, and the suspects replied they did not know their lights were out. Hall asked them where they were from, and one of the men said they were from Greenwich.

The suspect on the passenger side exited the vehicle during the conversation and shot Hall, according to Burnside. The suspect's muzzle flash temporarily blinded Burnside. Burnside said he was on the opposite side of the car from the shooter, so he ran around and opened fire multiple times, possibly striking the suspect. The driver yelled, "What's the matter?" The shooter said, "Oh my god!" in response, and staggered into the car while being pulled in by the driver, who sped away.[2]

Every available police officer responded once word of the shooting reached police headquarters. Hall's body was examined by the City Undertaking Company. The autopsy revealed a bullet had traveled through Hall's right breast and struck his lung.[3]

About twenty-four hours after the murder, Patrolman Charlie Clark, Patrolman J. W. Nickum, and Patrolman L. M. Fuget arrested nineteen-year-old Virgil Stotts and twenty-one-year-old J. E. Gaylor, at 21st Street and Lawrence Avenue (now Broadway Avenue). They were in a similar vehicle that the suspects were in and were reported to be in possession of ammunition and a firearm. However, the firearm found in their possession was the wrong caliber. The young males indicated they were in Kansas City and were headed back to Oklahoma City. Detective Burnside later said the two males were not the suspects.

Several vacant homes throughout the city were raided within twenty-four hours after the murder in hopes of finding a wounded suspect who was hiding from law enforcement. Detective Burnside indicated he believed he shot the suspect during the incident, so the police were searching for a wounded male. Their search discovered no such thing.[4]

Within two days after the murder, law enforcement received hopeful information about two men. One, the supposed driver, was formerly from Wichita, and the shooter was said to be visiting the city and had never lived in Wichita. The shooter's description

---

2. "Detective Hall Killed in Battle with Two Bandits," *The Wichita Eagle*, April 10, 1925.

3. "Detective Hall Killed," *Wichita Eagle*.

4. "Arrest 2 Men as Suspects in the Slaying of Hall," *The Wichita Eagle*, April 11, 1925.

given by Burnside was thought to be identical to the man they received information about. The lead, initially thought to be the case solver, turned out to be a bad one.[5]

Four days after the murder, on Tuesday, April 14, 1925, officers arrested seventeen-year-old A. Y. Yarnall, of 722 South Pattie Avenue, as he exited the train at Union Station. At the time, the police believed Yarnall knew the identity of the shooter. Mrs. N. A. Yarnall, his mother, was also arrested for failing to bring her son to the police station as she promised the Chief of Detectives Robert L. Pryor.[6] Both the mother and son were released and cleared of any wrongdoing after Pryor interviewed them.[7]

Detective Burnside obtained little sleep during the week after his partner was murdered in the line of duty. He was required to work his normal twelve-hour shift, and, in addition, had to travel to Greenwich, Arkansas City, Newton, Lyons, Winfield, El Dorado, Augusta, and several other cities throughout the week attempting to identify prisoners held at those locations. He never identified the suspects.[8]

Flags were at half-staff and all the businesses in Hoisington were closed during Detective Hall's funeral service. Approximately 3,000 people attended the service, more than the population of the town. Detective Burnside was an honorary pallbearer.[9]

An El Dorado man named David Cain was arrested one week after Hall's murder in Valley Center. He was suffering from a gunshot wound to the abdomen and was brought to Wichita on the belief that he was the suspect. However, Burnside confirmed he was not the man. Police learned he was shot two weeks before the arrest by the Ponca City police chief during a raid. He made his way from Oklahoma back to Kansas by freight train without seeking any medical assistance.[10]

Struggling to identify the killer of Detective Hall over a month later, Chief of Police T. J. Thompson put out a reward poster offering $750 for information leading to the arrest and conviction of the murderer. The poster was dated May 22, 1925.

---

5. "Underworld 'Tip' Puts Local Police on Slayer's Trail, *The Wichita Eagle*, April 12, 1925.

6. "Youth Sought in the Hall Murder is Under Arrest," *The Wichita Eagle*, April 14, 1925.

7. "First Reward for Detective Slayer Offered Tuesday," *The Wichita Eagle*, April 15, 1925.

8. "Gets Little Sleep," *The Wichita Eagle*, April 17, 1925.

9. "3000 Attend Hall Funeral Services," *The Wichita Eagle*, April 16, 1925.

10. "Holding Wounded Man," *The Wichita Eagle*, April 18, 1925.

At 1:15 o'clock A. M., Friday, April 10th, 1925, Detective Edward W. Hall, of this Department, was shot and killed by two unknown bandits driving an old Ford Touring Car. Description of bandits is as follows: No. 1 White man, about 20 or 25 years of age; 5 feet, 7 or 8 inches tall, weight about 130 pounds, wore light suit and hat. No. 2 White man about 30 or 32 years of age; 5 feet, 10 inches tall; weight about 150 pounds, slim build, prominent brown eyes, sharp features, looked like dope fiend. The above described men were driving on Hillside Avenue, without lights. Detectives Hall and Burnside stopped them calling their attention to the fact that they were driving without lights. After a short conversation the men in the car opened fire on the officers, killing Detective Hall at the first shot. Detective Burnside returned the fire and is believed to have wounded one of the bandits. Detective Hall was killed by a 38 caliber special bullet, copper jacket, probably fired from Colt 38 Special Revolver. The County Commissioners of Sedgwick County have offered a Reward of $500.00 for the arrest and conviction of the slayers of Detective E. W. Hall. The Governor of Kansas has also offered a reward of $250.00 for the arrest and conviction. Communicate any information to undersigned.[11]

Susan Hall, who was twenty-seven years old, suffered from shock and a broken heart at the passing of her husband. She was unable to attend his funeral and underwent three separate medical operations. Her health was in critical condition, then started to improve about two weeks before her death. She unexpectedly died on Friday, June 26, 1925, just before she was going to leave the hospital.[12]

As months passed, life became more difficult for Dick Burnside. Many people started to doubt his account of the murder, while some believed he took part in it. However, he never wavered from the details of his story, and he worked many hours on the case to identify the suspects. He was promoted for his efforts soon after the murder but was reduced to patrolman during one of the many "shake-ups" of the Department near the end of 1925. On January 22, 1926, he was fired from the Wichita Police Department.

---

11. Wichita Police Department, "Reward: Wanted for Murder," May 22, 1925.

12. "Officer's Widow Dies," *The Wichita Eagle*, June 28, 1925.

Soon after his termination, Burnside became ill and was transported to the hospital. In a desperate attempt to save his life, three blood transfusions were given to him. Complications from surgery for appendicitis, a very lethal medical problem back then, and pneumonia, caused his death on Friday, April 9, 1926, 364 days after the death of his partner.[13]

Wichita Police Chief T. J. Thompson left the Department in March of 1926, not long before Burnside died. Chief I. B. Walston, from Kansas City, became Chief in April of 1926 and served until March of 1928.

A few months after Walston started, an arrest was made in the case. Ed Smith, a former Wichita police motorcycle patrolman, was arrested in Los Angeles on July 14, 1926, for the murder of Detective Hall. The deputy marshal of city court, Frank Crow, and his assistant, Frank Bush, traveled to California to bring Smith back to Wichita after a warrant for his arrest was signed. The parties met for the preliminary hearing in Wichita on August 5, 1926, and Smith's first trial started on December 8, ultimately ending in a hung jury on December 13, 1926.[14]

During the first trial, Ross McCormick, special prosecutor, argued that Ed Smith was the man who fired the shot that killed Detective Hall near the entrance of the cemetery. In response, defense attorney Tom Harley attacked the police force and claimed the administration of the police department was trying to send an innocent man to prison "with a manufactured plot." Harley asked, "Is Walston, the big man from Kansas City, trying to add to his luster? Is he trying to put another star in his crown of glory?"[15]

During closing arguments, Judge D. A. Banta, arguing for the prosecution, spoke for forty-five minutes. He claimed that newspaper reporter Walter Kiser's story of being invited by Hall and Burnside to a wild party on the night of the murder was absurd and unbelievable. Banta said Smith was not a good person and pointed out Smith's own admissions as being someone "who went about with a hide full of moonshine."[16] Banta claimed Smith went to the morgue the day following Hall's murder so others would not be suspicious of him. He pointed out that Smith curiously asked Patrolman Harry Bowman about the Hall case and if the police had any idea who the suspect was.

---

13. "Burnside Passes Just Year After Companion Slain," *The Wichita Eagle*, April 9, 1926.

14. "Accused Killer of E. W. Hall On Way to Wichita," *The Wichita Eagle*, July 20, 1926.

15. "4 Hours Without Verdict," *The Wichita Eagle*, December 11, 1926.

16. "4 Hours," *Wichita Eagle*.

J. W. Ward, Smith's chief counsel and friend, followed Banta with his own arguments and started with criticism of Chief Walston and his failure to investigate Kiser's statement. He discredited the testimony of Patrolman Nickum and claimed Harry Bowman failed to do his duty as a police officer if Smith made suspicious inquiries regarding the Hall murder, as Bowman claimed during testimony. According to Ward, the testimonies of D. M. Hammers and Walter Raymond, employees of Lahey and Martin Mortuary, who overhead conversations involving Smith, were unreliable and contradicting.

Following Ward for the defense was Jim Conley, who referred to Private Detective Jack Drury as a "graveyard detective" that any person could buy any testimony from. Drury was hired by Hall's father and father-in-law to investigate his death. After Conley spoke, Tom Harley attacked Chief Walston's supervision of the case, claiming his personal ambition led to improper handling of the investigation.

The witness that helped Smith's case the most was Myrta Ringwald, who lived at 1457 North Lawrence Avenue at the time. She testified that she picked up Smith around 1930 hours from a drug store at 13th Street and Saint Francis Avenue, and they drove around the evening before the homicide. They drove to the Swallow flying field so Smith could apply for a job, and then they drove downtown to meet Ringwald's friend, but Ringwald was late, and the friend had already left. She brought Smith home with her for the rest of the night and drove him home in the morning. She indicated she was afraid Smith would get into trouble if he stayed downtown that night, and that he did not look very well. During cross-examination, Harry Castor pointed out discrepancies between her testimony and the statements she gave Chief Walston in the past.[17]

Smith calmly took the stand and presented the same story that Ringwald told. He denied shooting Hall, discussed various animosities within the police force, and admitted that he disliked Hall. He believed Hall tried to get him fired from the police department. One day, they were both drinking alcohol from the same bottle at Sim Park. Smith overheard that Hall had been at the sheriff's office not long before. Hall excused himself and left the park, which Smith thought was suspicious. A short time later, Sheriff Chet Conner, Detective Roy Criswell, and a third male drove up, as if they were trying to catch him drinking alcohol. In response, Smith admitted that he tried to get Hall fired after that.

Smith indicated he went to the morgue and saw Hall's body the morning he was killed. He saw Hammers and Raymond, employees of the mortuary, but he did not see

---

17. "4 Hours Without Verdict," *The Wichita Eagle*, December 11, 1926.

Harry Bowman. He claimed he never saw Bowman at the mortuary in February or March of 1925, and denied making threats about "getting Hall," as Bowman testified to earlier.[18]

During the second and final trial regarding the murder, prosecutors used three new witnesses in attempt to add credibility to Patrolman Nickum's testimony of the arrest of Ed Smith during a raid that led to his dismissal from the Wichita Police Department, months before Detective Hall's murder.

Detective Hall participated in the raid of Velma Patton's apartment at 18th Street and Lawrence Avenue, which prosecutors claimed was Smith's motive for the murder of Hall. Velma Patton Baumgardner and Edna Brown, both residents of the apartment, testified that Smith was there at a wild party. The third witness, W. H. Wright, a Southwestern Bell Telephone Company employee, contradicted himself several times and seemed confused. The prosecutors were unable to establish that Smith was at the apartment for a lengthy amount of time before his arrest for a liquor charge.

Patrolman Nickum testified during both trials that Smith and a woman were found naked in a room together. However, Patrolman George Jones testified that during the raid, Smith was fully dressed and found in a room with no woman. Also with Jones were Hall, Walter Rambo, and Burnside. This contradiction was highlighted heavily by Smith's defense attorneys during the first trial.

Nickum's testimony during the second trial was of great interest to everyone. While walking the 18th Street and Lawrence Avenue beat, he observed officers go into Fairview Apartments and decided to follow them in. As in the first trial, he testified that Hall forced open the door to the apartment where Smith was arrested. However, Jones said the door was opened with a pass key that was obtained by the manager. According to Nickum, Smith told Hall, "I'll get you sooner or later." Nickum said Smith and the woman, who he did not know, were naked.[19]

A former police officer and a Coleman Lamp Company employee, Gerald Bodkin, testified that he was at the police station (as an officer at the time) when Smith was brought in by officers just after the raid. While the two were getting a drink of water, according to Bodkin, Smith told him, "I'll have to get even with Nibs (Detective Hall)." Bodkin

---

18. "4 Hours Without Verdict," *The Wichita Eagle*, December 11, 1926.

19. "Three Surprise Witnesses Tell of 'Wild Party,'" *The Wichita Eagle*, March 9, 1927.

was later dismissed from the police department, and at the time of his testimony, he was hoping to be rehired by the Department, which was pointed out by the defense.[20]

Walter Raymond testified again about Smith's remark at the morgue that "Hall won't snitch on anyone else." D. M. Hammers took the stand and talked about Smith making a threat regarding Hall in the presence of Harry Bowman before Hall was murdered. Bowman then testified and discussed the threat and mentioned Smith contacting him one morning after the murder near the Bitting building. During the conversation, Smith talked to him about the same threat and said that he brought a load of alcohol from Kansas City on the night of the murder.

During the first trial, Bowman said Chief Walston was the first person he told of the conversation. However, during the second trial, Bowman said he told "Tex" Thompson, the chief at the time, about it. Thompson informed him that plain clothes detectives would handle the case and that he should mind his business.[21]

Patrolman L. A. Jarvis testified Smith told him that he was drunk inside his home, which was about a half block away from the murder, when Burnside came over just after the killing, seeking a telephone to report the incident. A phone was not installed at the house yet, because Smith recently moved to the residence. Multiple officers and former officers testified about Smith making comments about framing Hall and getting him fired.[22]

The only part of the trial that was considered direct testimony came from Private Detective Drury, the man hired by Hall's father and father-in-law. Drury claimed he was near Smith's house, concealed near the rear steps, close enough to hear a conversation between Smith and Burnside. Drury testified that he heard Smith tell Burnside, "Why don't you put him under a marble slab where I put Hall?" According to Drury, Smith was referring to another private detective that Burnside was worried about.[23]

During closing arguments, Wertz, the county attorney, said Smith moved to a house about two hundred feet from the cemetery not long before the murder. He believed that Burnside brought Hall to the cemetery, so Smith could kill him while Smith hid behind the hedge fence.

---

20. "Three Surprise Witnesses Tell of 'Wild Party,'" *The Wichita Eagle*, March 9, 1927.

21. "Three Surprise Witnesses," *Wichita Eagle*.

22. "Three Surprise Witnesses," *Wichita Eagle*.

23. "Sealed Verdict is Returned in Ed Smith Trial," *The Wichita Eagle*, March 11, 1927.

For the defense, J. W. Ward argued that Smith had just as much reason to kill Burnside, Rambo, and Jones because they were a part of the raid. He claimed Nickum's testimony was not credible and was contradictory to Rambo and Jones' testimonies. Ward said Drury was a private detective who only cared about getting the reward money for Hall's murder. Harley followed Ward and talked about the danger of second-hand statements and how they can be misconstrued. He said even the prosecutors claimed the police force was no good under Chief Thompson. Harley pointed out that a lot of the same men still work there, so it is no different under Chief Walston.[24]

Ed Smith was found not guilty by the jury on Friday, March 11, 1927.[25] The two trials put the Wichita Police Department on center stage, and the entire city observed the disorder. Like in 1888, the organization had many challenges and deficiencies during this period.

---

24. "Sealed Verdict is Returned in Ed Smith Trial," *The Wichita Eagle*, March 11, 1927.

25. "Acquit Ex-Policeman," *The Emporia Gazette*, March 11, 1927.

14

PATROLMAN VERNON E. OGDEN

Date: June 26, 1927
Day: Accident occurred on Saturday - Died on Sunday
Time: Accident occurred at 1345 hours - Died at approximately 0700 hours
Location: At the Frisco tracks and Cleveland Avenue (south of 1001 North Cleveland Avenue)
Tour: Three months (1927)
Age: Twenty-three
Race: White
Gender: Male
Marital Status: Married
Military Veteran: Unknown
Children: One
Badge: Not applicable
Burial: Wichita Park Cemetery and Mausoleum, Wichita, Sedgwick County, Kansas
Cause: Vehicle pursuit
Weapon: Not applicable
Offender Status: Not applicable
Offender Age: Not applicable
Offender Race: Not applicable
Offender Gender: Not applicable
Chief of Police at the Time: I. B. Walston

Patrolman Vernon E. Ogden. Wichita Police Department.

Patrolman Vernon E. Ogden, who was on a motorcycle, was injured in a vehicle accident at 1345 hours on Saturday, June 25, 1927, as he was trying to catch up to a speeder near the Frisco tracks on North Cleveland Avenue. He died the next day at Saint Francis Hospital at approximately 0700 hours. The driver of the car that Ogden was attempting to stop was J. B. Wolf, who lived in Fairchild Apartments. The passenger in the vehicle was C. B. Stockstill, who indicated to police that he and Wolf had no idea that the patrolman was pursuing them when Wolf decided to beat the train while driving south on Cleveland Avenue.[1]

The primary witness in this case was Chester Kimel, the owner of the drug store that was located at 1001 North Cleveland Avenue. He told Chief Walston that Wolf and Stockstill were originally north on Cleveland Avenue. Stockstill was a car salesman who was hoping to sell the car to Wolf at the time. Ogden, who was on duty, entered the store and asked Kimel to put some iodine on a cut finger. While Ogden was inside the store, he spotted Wolf and Stockstill's vehicle driving quickly south on Cleveland Avenue. Ogden hurried to his motorcycle to stop them.

---

1. "War Declared on Wichita Speeders when Ogden Dies," *The Wichita Eagle*, June 26, 1927.

Kimel also went outside to watch from the middle of the street. He observed the car clear the tracks just before the Frisco passenger train crossed Cleveland Avenue. Ogden swerved his motorcycle to his left and attempted to bail from it, but the rear wheel struck the train causing the machine and Ogden to be flung into the air and strike a curb. Forty feet of skid marks were located on the pavement.

Ogden remained unconscious, clenching both hands and occasionally had seizures until he died the next morning. Chief Walston believed, based on the evidence, that Ogden was driving sixty miles per hour when the accident occurred. The officer sustained a broken leg, a crushed skull and chest, and a gash on his side.[2]

Following the accident, there was a large amount of speculation regarding the wig-wag signal and whether it was working when the crash occurred. Arch E. Hardy, a claim agent for the Frisco Railroad, investigated the matter. He learned from multiple witnesses that several motorists were halted by the signal on the other side of the tracks, so he concluded the signal was operational.[3]

A lot of animosity toward speeders flowed through the community and the Department following the death of Patrolman Ogden. A statement issued by Chief Walston on the day Ogden died is evidence of these widely held feelings:

> "Too much speeding and too much reckless driving," the chief declared. "It must stop. This is a terrible example of the consequences that are all too frequent. I'm going to see if we can't get heavier fines for offenders. We ought to have a jail sentence for them, too. Other cities have."[4]

An article in *The Wichita Beacon*, prompted by Ogden's death, pointed out that a safe speed to operate a vehicle on the average city street was fifteen to twenty miles per hour, a belief that would not be very popular in today's world. Also contained in this article was the following: "The Evening Eagle does not know – or pretend to know – where the responsibility lies for the death of Policeman Ogden. But it does know as does everyone, that a motor-car operated at a speed past possibility of full stop within a distance

---

2. "War Declared on Wichita Speeders when Ogden Dies," *The Wichita Eagle*, June 26, 1927.

3. "Signal at Fatal Crossing Working, Says Investigator," *The Wichita Beacon*, June 30, 1927.

4. "War Declared," *Wichita Eagle*.

of a few feet constitutes that condition known in the language of the street as 'flirting with death.'"[5]

Ogden's family members decided not to seek prosecution against J. B. Wolfe for speeding and reckless driving. His case was dropped by the city on Friday, July 8, 1927. George Jones, the court clerk, indicated that there were multiple witnesses who claim that Wolfe was not speeding at the time of the accident, so a conviction would have been unlikely.[6]

Patrolman Vernon E. Ogden had a six-month-old baby named Laverna when he died. He was survived by her, his wife, Ima Ogden, and his parents.[7] He was laid to rest on Tuesday, June 28, 1927, at Wichita Park Cemetery, located at 3424 East 21st Street.[8] Among the pallbearers were Sergeant E. Motley, Sergeant C. P. Wilder, J. J. Myler, Paul Palmer, and J. O. Pugh.[9]

---

5. "In the Crucible," *The Wichita Beacon*, June 27, 1927.

6. "Driver of Machine Involved in Fatal Accident Cleared," *The Wichita Beacon*, July 9, 1927.

7. "War Declared on Wichita Speeders when Ogden Dies," *The Wichita Eagle*, June 26, 1927.

8. "Motorcycle Officer Laid to Rest," *The Wichita Beacon*, June 28, 1927.

9. "Mile-long Procession," *The Wichita Eagle*, June 29, 1927.

15

Patrolman Joseph E. Marshall

Date: August 29, 1927
Day: Monday
Time: Shot at 0200 hours - Died at 0327 hours
Location: 1100 North Lawrence Avenue (now Broadway Avenue)
Tour: Two years, one month (1925-1927)
Age: Twenty-eight
Race: White
Gender: Male
Marital Status: Married
Military Veteran: Unknown
Children: Two
Badge: Not applicable
Burial: Wichita Park Cemetery and Mausoleum, Wichita, Sedgwick County, Kansas
Cause: Gunfire
Weapon: .45 caliber handgun
Offender Status: Committed suicide
Offender Age: Thirty-three
Offender Race: White
Offender Gender: Male
Chief of Police at the Time: I. B. Walston

Patrolman Joseph E. Marshall. Wichita Police Department.

Motorcycle Patrolman Joseph E. Marshall was fatally shot after he and his partner, Frank Bush, stopped a Chevrolet sedan at 1100 North Lawrence Avenue (now Broadway Avenue) on August 29, 1927, at approximately 0200 hours. He was transported by a Lahey and Martin ambulance to Saint Francis Hospital nearby where he died at 0327 hours.[1] The three occupants of the vehicle had robbed the Crystal Ice plant in

---

1. "Two Trails of Blood Lead Officers to Believe All 3 Wounded by Pal of Victim," *The Wichita Eagle*, August 29, 1927.

Newton, Kansas a short time before. Officers in Wichita were given orders to investigate all vehicles on the road after the robbery occurred.[2]

The details of the incident mostly came from Frank Bush, who was riding in the sidecar of Marshall's motorcycle when they stopped the three suspects. Bush indicated the following: Marshall and Bush were covering their beat around 0200 hours when they turned south on Lawrence Avenue. A Chevrolet sedan with a Kansas tag caught their eyes because it appeared to be speeding.[3] "We saw nothing unusual in the car. . . . It passed us. We were talking about the weather, congratulating ourselves that we were not riding in the rain as we had been the night before. We had just telephoned our report to the station. We took after the speeding car."[4]

Bush asked Marshall how fast they were going, and his reply was forty miles per hour. They caught up to the vehicle around the 1100 block of North Lawrence Avenue. "'Pull over to the curb,' Marshall said, after we had turned the spotlight on them. They obeyed and there was nothing suspicious looking about their actions, nothing out of the ordinary in any way."[5]

Marshall got off his motorcycle first and made contact on the driver's side of the vehicle while holding his handgun down near his side. He poked his head into the door window. Bush approached the passenger side of the vehicle after he drew his gun. Bush observed the driver, a small, tanned white male, reach out and grab Marshall as he raised a gun towards Marshall's head. A physical fight ensued between Marshall and the driver. As this occurred, a male exited the back seat with a gun and ran west through a lawn.

As the chaos unfolded, Bush fired multiple shots at the man who was running and observed him fall to the ground. It was unclear to Bush at the time if he wounded the running suspect, but the man fired shots in return at Bush after he fell.[6]

---

2. "Wichita Officer Slain by Bandits," *The Manhattan Mercury*, August 27, 1927.

3. "Fugitive Bandit Eludes Police Net," *The Wichita Eagle*, August 29, 1927.

4. "Bandit Killer's Wish for Larger Gun to be Realized Today in a New $50 Pistol," *The Wichita Eagle*, September 1, 1927.

5. "Bandit Killer's Wish," *Wichita Eagle*.

6. "Fugitive Bandit," *Wichita Eagle*.

I thought I had him sure, when he went down, but he kept shooting so I turned loose another one or two and then ran over to where Barker [the driver] had a headlock on Marshall while he was firing into Marshall's face. Jamming my gun right up to him, I ripped out a curse at him. I couldn't help it. Then I pulled the trigger [Bush's last round]. A forty-five would have paralyzed him. As Marshall slumped into my arms, I pulled out my sap and struck Barker. Then Marshall eased to the ground and the car drove away.[7]

The last round that Bush fired struck Barker. The suspect vehicle fled south on Lawrence Avenue to Pine Street and went east toward Saint Francis Avenue. The wounded Barker swerved into a muddy ditch, struck a telephone post, and came to a rest against a tree along Pine Street, near Saint Francis Avenue. Bush, back at the scene, picked up Marshall, who was still breathing, and laid him in the grass and went to find some help.[8]

After hearing the crash of the suspect vehicle, citizens observed two people exiting the vehicle and travel in opposite directions. The driver staggered north across Pine Street and fell into the weeds while groaning. They then heard one gunshot when the driver shot himself.[9] It was later learned that the driver fired a .45 caliber bullet through his right temple, which probably killed him instantly. The front seat passenger, who was believed to be injured by gunfire, was nowhere to be seen. The citizen's call to police occurred before Bush reached a phone to call for help.[10]

While the initial police response did not locate the front seat passenger, Motorcycle Sergeant Jimmy Pugh, Patrolman George Travis, Patrolman Jake Kanack, and Patrolman A. P. Hathaway conducted a thorough search of the immediate area after the sun rose, when Kanack spotted the suspect's shoes and head sticking out from a tall patch of weeds not far to the southeast from where the vehicle wrecked. A short blood trail led Kanack to the discovery, and upon finding him, he conversed with the wounded man to see if he was still alive and armed. An ambulance transported the man, Charles Stallcup, to the

---

7. "Bandit Killer's Wish for Larger Gun to be Realized Today in a New $50 Pistol," *The Wichita Eagle*, September 1, 1927.

8. "Fugitive Bandit Eludes Police Net," *The Wichita Eagle*, August 29, 1927.

9. "Bitter Fight is Being Waged for a Stallcup Jury," *The Wichita Eagle*, November 1, 1927.

10. "Fugitive Bandit," *Wichita Eagle*.

nearby Saint Francis Hospital, where he was treated for gunshot wounds to his right arm and both legs.

Lt. Clyde Wilder and Chief Walston spoke with Stallcup and learned that he served time in Lansing for a burglary he committed in Newton, and he also served time at McAlester Penitentiary in Oklahoma. He indicated that he and the other two suspects, whom he identified as Barker and "Myers," committed the robbery in Newton. Stallcup said Barker was driving the vehicle and killed the police officer. He denied doing any of the shooting and said he met up with Barker and "Myers" in Coffeyville three days prior. Stallcup told Chief Walston that he stayed at the New Wellington Hotel in room number thirty-seven while in Wichita. Officers went there and confirmed that he registered the room under the name of Charley Andrews and checked out sometime during Sunday afternoon.

The vehicle used by the suspects was registered out of Dodge City to Helen West and believed by law enforcement to be stolen. The manager of the Crystal Ice company, T. E. Reiff, and the attendant that was working at the time of the robbery, Raymond Moulds, came to Wichita an hour after the gunbattle. Moulds went to Gill Mortuary and identified Barker as the primary suspect in the robbery in Newton and indicated he wore the same clothing. He said the two other men had on masks, but Barker did not. Barker locked him in the ice chamber. Moulds said Barker "was the man with the nerve."[11]

Moulds shared his account of the robbery in Newton while he was at the mortuary:

> After midnight things had slowed up at the plant and Mr. Reiff had left. I was there all alone when these three men came in about 12:45. Two of them were masked, one wearing a black mask and the other wearing a white one. This man (pointing to the body) was unmasked and he held a big automatic pistol on me. The men were puttering around the big safe, unloading their burglary tools, when one of them shouted, "It's about time to get rid of that guy!" The small man then made me show him the ice chamber and put me inside. I begged him to give me a coat of some kind and they threw me a raincoat. They told me to keep my mouth shut and then I could hear 'em going about their work. All the other doors to the ice chamber were closed and they shut the front door by barring it

---

11. "Fugitive Bandit Eludes Police Net," *The Wichita Eagle*, August 29, 1927.

with a punch from their tools.... I could hear 'em battering around for perhaps 30 minutes. Then everything grew quiet. I heard a car drive off and I began trying to get out. It took me about 30 minutes more to get free. I found a crowbar used to push ice around in the chamber. I pried some screws off a side door and got out. The hour in the chamber had chilled badly [sic]. I called my employer and then we called the officers in Newton and later the officers in Wichita. In the 30 minutes the bandits worked, they hacked off the iron door to the vault, an inner door and the door to the safe. They also had to get through an inner safe door. They must have worked with the smoothness of experienced cracksmen. They took two sacks of money containing as far as we can figure about $100 in cash and $100 in checks. I had a considerable amount of cash I had taken in during the night in my pocket, but they didn't touch that.[12]

Officers seized a very elaborate burglary tool kit from the suspect vehicle, along with two sacks of money. A .38 caliber automatic and a .32 caliber automatic were also seized, and officers believed that one of the guns belonged to Patrolman Marshall who may have dropped it in the car when he was shot. The suspect vehicle had multiple bullet strikes, and Stallcup's wounds may have been caused by the fleeing "Myers" when he tried to shoot Patrolman Bush, or by Patrolman Marshall when he struggled with Barker.[13] Detectives believed that after Marshall was shot in the head, but before he fell to the ground, Marshall fired one shot from his gun.[14]

Marshall appeared to have been shot four times. One round entered his left temple and exited the right side of his head, and the other three rounds struck his right eye, mouth, and left elbow. In addition to Barker's self-inflicted head wound, a bullet traveled through his right breast, caused by Bush, and a wound to his left arm, possibly caused by himself when he shot Marshall. Barker was a small man with dark hair, a beard, and several tattoos, including one of a nude woman on his right arm. At the time of his death, he was wearing a dark blue suit with a red checked pattern.

---

12. "Fugitive Bandit Eludes Police Net," *The Wichita Eagle*, August 29, 1927.

13. "Fugitive Bandit," *Wichita Eagle*.

14. "Bitter Fight is Being Waged for a Stallcup Jury," *The Wichita Eagle*, November 1, 1927.

Marie Marshall, the patrolman's wife, made it to his side before he passed away at Saint Francis Hospital in the infirmary. They lived at 421 North Kansas Avenue with their two sons, six-year-old Luther Edwin Marshall and four-year-old Marvin Logan Marshall. Patrolman Marshall's employment with the Wichita Police Department started on July 7, 1925. He was known for his calm demeanor in stressful situations.[15]

The third suspect, who Charley Stallcup identified as "Myers," turned out to be Porter Meeks. Meeks hid out in a patch of tall weeds near 20th Street and Waco Avenue and only left for food and drink. He entered the Watts and Son grocery store at 2255 North Jackson Avenue, where Mrs. Nina Watts worked, during the morning of Wednesday, August 31, 1927. Mrs. Watts developed a suspicious feeling about Meeks, who was armed with a handgun in his belt, so she notified the police station by phone after Meeks purchased a bottle of near beer and left the store.[16] Harold Burkholder, a brave fourteen-year-old boy, trailed Meeks.

Detectives Merle Colver, Dan Carrier, Lekron, and Maness responded to Mrs. Watts' call and encountered Burkholder, who indicated he could point out the house the suspicious man went to. Burkholder hopped in the police vehicle. The boy identified a vacant house near Wichita Street and 26th Street. Carrier, Lekron, and Maness went to the rear of the residence.

Colver went to the front and spotted Meeks on the north side of the house, displayed his badge and unholstered his gun, and told the suspect to stop. At the time, Colver inaccurately believed he was talking to Elmer Inman, a notorious member of the same gang as Meeks. Meeks stopped and raised his hands, then grabbed for his gun and opened fire. The first round entered the police car and struck Burkholder's leg, causing a minor wound. The subsequent two rounds hit the rear door of the police car. Colver's first round struck Meeks in the side, two misfired, one missed, and the final round entered Meeks' heart. He died before reaching the hospital.[17]

Meeks' fingerprints were wired to McAlester Penitentiary staff, who identified him. He had an extensive criminal record and was a fugitive from justice in Oklahoma. Meeks was convicted of robbery in 1914 in Payne County, Oklahoma, and highway robbery in

---

15. "Fugitive Bandit Eludes Police Net," *The Wichita Eagle*, August 29, 1927.

16. Near beer was a malt beverage that had a very low alcohol content. It was legally sold in the United States during the Prohibition era.

17. "Death in Hunch of a Woman," *The Wichita Eagle*, September 1, 1927.

1919 in Dallas, Texas. Officers learned that he only suffered from a bruised knee during the initial gunfight with Patrolman Bush the previous Monday, and he shot twice at Bush using a .45 caliber pistol. He used the same gun during the gunfight with Detective Colver.

Barker was later identified by the Wichita Police Department as Herman Barker. His body was transported to Miami, Oklahoma a few days after his death so his relatives could give him a decent burial. He was thirty-three years old when he died.[18]

Not long after the tragedy, fellow officers purchased a blue steel .45 caliber Colt pistol for Bush, which cost $50. They did this out of respect for Bush's actions during the incident, and they knew he wanted one for the job.[19]

County Attorney W. J. Wertz, during Stallcup's trial, claimed that Stallcup said the .45 caliber gun that police found with Barker, after he committed suicide, belonged to Stallcup. The prosecution argued that Stallcup was an active participant in the gunbattle, and not a passive witness that the defense claimed. Expert testimony was provided during the trial that indicated that at least one of Marshall's head wounds was caused by a round similar in size to a .45 caliber.[20]

Charles Stallcup was convicted of first-degree murder. His chief defense attorney during the trial was I. H. Stallcup, his father, who was from Picher, Oklahoma.[21] It was Bush, sworn in as deputy sheriff by C. E. Grove, who was given the honor of transporting Stallcup to Lansing Penitentiary with the approval of Chief Walston. He was transported on January 5, 1928.[22]

---

18. "Death in Hunch of a Woman," *The Wichita Eagle*, September 1, 1927.

19. "Bandit Killer's Wish for Larger Gun to be Realized Today in a New $50 Pistol," *The Wichita Eagle*, September 1, 1927.

20. "Trying to Prove Stallcup's Gun Killed Marshall," *The Wichita Eagle*, November 3, 1927.

21. "New Court Record Set as Ossweiler Verdict Returned," *The Wichita Eagle*, November 28, 1927.

22. "Wichita Man Who Shot it out with Bandit Trio Will Take Survivor to State Pen Today," *The Wichita Eagle*, January 5, 1928.

16

SERGEANT PAUL E. GILMORE

Date: June 18, 1930
Day: Died on Friday
Time: Died at 1215 hours
Location: Wichita Hospital (Douglas Avenue and Seneca Street)
Tour: Eleven years (1919-1930)
Age: Thirty-two
Race: White
Gender: Male
Marital Status: Married
Military Veteran: Yes - Army
Children: Three
Badge: Not applicable
Burial: Maple Grove Cemetery, Wichita, Sedgwick County, Kansas
Cause: Motorcycle crash
Weapon: Not applicable
Offender Status: Not applicable
Offender Age: Not applicable
Offender Race: Not applicable
Offender Gender: Not applicable
Chief of Police at the Time: O. W. Wilson

Sergeant Paul E. Gilmore. Wichita Police Department.

Sergeant Paul E. Gilmore was given the title "Hard Luck Champ" in May of 1930 by members of the Wichita Police Department and *The Wichita Beacon* due to his misfortune of accidents and medical operations that he experienced. Chief Orlando Wilson referred to him as the "grittiest fellow on the force" because Gilmore kept working for the Department after receiving some of his injuries.[1] They did not know at the time that Gilmore would no longer be with them in less than two months after giving him the name.

About nine months before his death, during the morning hours of Saturday, September 21, 1929, Gilmore sustained multiple fractures in his left leg, dislocated a thumb, and suffered additional injuries when he struck a truck at Central and Bluff Avenue. He was attempting to catch up to a speeder, traveling at approximately sixty-two miles per hour, when he struck another vehicle and was thrown over thirty feet into a fire hydrant. The driver of the truck (but not the speeder) was H. C. Baland, who was twenty-three years old at the time, and was attempting to make a left turn at the intersection. Gilmore attempted to avoid the truck but ended up striking the left fender and destroyed the motorcycle.[2]

---

1. "Cop Claims Title 'Hard Luck Champ,'" *The Wichita Eagle*, May 6, 1930.

2. "Cop Chasing Speeder Hurt," *The Wichita Eagle*, September 21, 1929.

"Gillie," who many people called him, spent six weeks in a cast after the initial operation. While his leg healed, he worked in the record office. He attempted to walk after the cast was removed but could not do so without his crutches. During the second operation, part of his bone was removed. After recovering from this operation, he went back to work on his motorcycle.[3]

Sometime between the end of April or the beginning of May in 1930, Gilmore somehow cut the artery in his right leg, above his ankle. *The Wichita Eagle* did not specify how this occurred. However, the newspaper indicated that while Gilmore was at the doctor's office being treated, a citizen ran into his motorcycle and damaged the transmission. Gilmore had to pay eleven dollars to get it fixed.

On Friday, June 13, 1930, as Gilmore was in the process of recovering from a third operation, he suffered a severe case of appendicitis that was believed to be associated with his initial accident. He had made significant progress after the third operation and felt he was reaching a level close to normalcy regarding his legs.[4]

On Wednesday, June 18, 1930, at 1215 hours, after a second operation regarding the appendicitis and peritonitis, Sergeant Paul Gilmore died the day after his thirty-second birthday. He was the son of M. A. "Pap" Gilmore, who was one of the oldest patrolmen in the Department.

Gilmore organized the Junior Patrol, which was responsible for keeping children safe at street crossings near schools. He was beloved by hundreds of students throughout the city. Chief Wilson said he was a very effective traffic officer: "He was the type who never arrested when he thought a warning would do as much good. I never had a report on him talking back, or getting tough."[5] Evidence of his popularity was observed when citizens organized a dance ball at the Ritz to raise proceeds for a new motorcycle for Gilmore on Monday, October 7, 1929, not long after the initial crash.[6]

On Tuesday, September 2, 1930, the city commissioners voted in favor of giving Mrs. Gilmore a pension equaling half of the pay Sergeant Gilmore was drawing monthly at the time of his death. Evidence and testimony were provided by family members,

---

3. "Most Popular Officer Dies," *The Wichita Beacon*, June 18, 1930.

4. "Hard Luck Dogs Cop," *The Wichita Eagle*, June 14, 1930.

5. "Most Popular Officer," *Wichita Beacon*.

6. "Benefit Dance at the Ritz for Officer Hurt in Line of Duty Here," *The Wichita Eagle*, October 3, 1929.

associates, and physicians that Gilmore never returned to normal health after the accident, and the injuries he received may have contributed to his appendicitis.[7]

Gilmore joined the Department in 1919, not long after the end of World War I. He had plans to become a doctor, but an argument with a professor at Friends University caused him to be expelled and barred from other universities. He lived at 120 South Saint Clair Street with his wife and three children.[8]

---

7. "Widow of Policeman Allowed Pension of Half Husband's Pay," *The Wichita Eagle*, September 3, 1930.

8. "Most Popular Officer Dies," *The Wichita Beacon*, June 18, 1930.

17

Lieutenant James O. Pugh

Date: July 31, 1930
Day: Accident on Sunday - Died on Thursday
Time: Accident at 2000 hours - Died at 2235 hours
Location: Near Highway Number 81 and 53rd Street
Tour: Four years, seven months (1926-1930)
Age: Thirty-nine to forty
Race: White
Gender: Male
Marital Status: Married
Military Veteran: Yes - Army
Children: One
Badge: Not applicable
Burial: Wichita Park Cemetery and Mausoleum, Wichita, Sedgwick County, Kansas
Cause: Motorcycle crash
Weapon: Not applicable
Offender Status: Not applicable
Offender Age: Not applicable
Offender Race: Not applicable
Offender Gender: Not applicable
Chief of Police at the Time: O. W. Wilson

Lieutenant James O. Pugh. Wichita Police Department.

Lieutenant James "Jimmie" Pugh was on his way to North Wichita, going south on Highway Number 81, after searching for the suspects who robbed businesses in Wichita, when he wrecked his motorcycle on Sunday, July 20, 1930, at 2000 hours.

During the accident, his right leg struck one of the fenders to a car causing a severe break. "The break was so bad that the bones protruded through his boot and his foot was doubled back against the front of his thigh when Lahey and Martin ambulance drivers found him."[1] To make matters worse, another motorcycle driver slammed into the wreckage.

The area to the north of Wichita was known as Wichita Heights. Pugh was transported to Saint Francis Hospital where his right leg was amputated below the knee. He suffered internal injuries and a broken right arm as well.

Before the accident, Pugh spent hours in the north end of Sedgwick County searching for the suspects who robbed the Miller and Palace theaters in Wichita. He was headed south on Highway Number 81 at a high rate of speed when a car backed onto the highway in front of him. Pugh attempted to swerve but was unsuccessful. After striking

---

1. "Crippled Cop Unaware of Loss," *The Wichita Eagle*, July 21, 1930.

the vehicle's fender, his new motorcycle that he had for two weeks fell on top of him. The second motorcycle rider struck the wreckage, causing that motorcycle to also fall onto Pugh.[2]

The threat of gangrene in Pugh's leg became a major concern on Tuesday, two days after the accident.[3] By Saturday, July 26, 1930, his condition was extremely serious, and a nurse told someone that Pugh had about a fifty percent chance of surviving. Doctors hoped that blood transfusions would help him, but he developed chills afterwards.[4]

He showed a temporary increase in strength on Sunday, a week after the accident.[5] Unfortunately, around midnight on Thursday, July 31, 1930, his muscles were becoming rigid and, by morning, his jaws were starting to lock.[6] He died later that night from tetanus at 2235 hours.[7]

Lieutenant James O. Pugh was hired by the Wichita Police Department on January 6, 1926. He was promoted to sergeant on August 22, 1927, and became the lieutenant over the traffic squad on February 1, 1928.[8] He was survived by his wife and six-year-old daughter, Evelyn Mae Pugh.[9]

---

2. "Lieut. Jimmie Pugh Loses Right Leg in Crash Near Wichita," *The Wichita Eagle*, July 21, 1930.

3. "Pugh Still in Danger," *The Wichita Eagle*, July 23, 1930.

4. "Injured Officer in Bad Condition," *The Wichita Eagle*, July 26, 1930.

5. "Pugh Much Improved," *The Wichita Eagle*, July 28, 1930.

6. "Lose Hope as Lockjaw Hits Jimmy Pugh," *The Wichita Eagle*, July 31, 1930.

7. "Wichita Mourns Death of Pugh," *The Wichita Eagle*, August 1, 1930.

8. "Lieut. Jimmie Pugh Dies of Tetanus Following Injuries," *Kansas Masonic Digest*, August 1, 1930.

9. "Wichita Mourns," *Wichita Eagle*.

18

Patrolman Merle R. Colver

Date: August 14, 1931
Day: Friday
Time: 0810 hours
Location: 108 ½ South Water Street, Room Fifteen
Tour: Seven years, seven months (1924-1931)
Age: Forty
Race: White
Gender: Male
Marital Status: Married
Military Veteran: No
Children: Two
Badge: Not applicable
Burial: Clearwater Cemetery, Clearwater, Sedgwick County, Kansas
Cause: Gunfire
Weapon: .45 caliber handgun
Offender Status: Convicted of murder
Offender Age: Twenty-nine
Offender Race: White
Offender Gender: Male
Chief of Police at the Time: O. W. Wilson

Patrolman Merle R. Colver. Wichita Police Department.

Patrolman Merle Colver was shot and killed when he contacted two robbery suspects who were staying in room number fifteen at the Iris Hotel at Douglas Avenue and Water Street on Friday, August 14, 1931, at 0810 hours. Several personal photographs were in the hotel room not far from where Colver's body was found that helped police develop two suspects early in the case. One of the suspects was twenty-nine-year-old Wilbur Underhill, who was an escaped killer from Oklahoma. He used the alias names of Robert and Ralph Caraway.

The room was registered to the name of Frank Vann. Police learned the same man who registered the room was also involved in a vehicle accident on South Lawrence Avenue (now Broadway Avenue) just after midnight on Friday, August 14, 1931, where he sustained some injuries to his head and leg. After the accident, he was treated at Wichita Hospital and gave employees the name of Frank Vance from Kansas City.[1]

A picture was located under Colver's body of a young woman. On the back of the photo was handwriting that said, "My favorite, Lucille Underhill." A business stamp on

---

1. "Merle Colver Shot Down by Bandit Pair in Hotel Here," *The Wichita Eagle*, August 14, 1931.

the back of the photo indicated the photo was printed in Heavener, Oklahoma. Detectives followed up with law enforcement in Heavener and learned Lucille was possibly the wife of Wilbur Underhill. A second photograph located at the crime scene showed another woman with writing that said, "Bertha Cannon, Ark. City, Kan." Police officials in Heavener said Bertha was Wilbur's sister. Detectives also learned that Wilbur escaped from an Oklahoma penitentiary a month prior to Colver's murder, after he received a life sentence for murdering a drug clerk during a robbery.

Chief O. W. Wilson's secretary, Lieutenant Harry Hoffman, tried to reconstruct what he believed occurred for reporters. He believed Colver went to the Iris Hotel at Douglas Avenue and Water Street and most likely read the names on the registry. There had been three robberies in or near the city involving filling stations, including one at Kellogg Avenue and Ida Street. Colver probably obtained descriptions for two strangers connected to the registry, which were like descriptions of the robbery suspects.

Hoffman speculated that Colver went to room fifteen, contacted two men, and lined them up to search them for weapons. During the process of searching or questioning the two suspects, one of the suspects shot and killed Colver.

Cora Botherton, the landlady of the hotel, heard a physical scuffle when Colver went to the room, then a gunshot. There was a pause after the gunshot, followed by three rapid gunshots. Officers later located four casings on the floor and learned one of the bullets traveled through a mattress and was located on the floor. Police believed Colver was shot with a .45 caliber semi-automatic pistol. His head was near the door and his feet were near the center of the small room. His body had powder burns.

One of the suspects threw a bloody shirt into room eighteen. The older suspect told Cora, "There has been an accident, better call the police." The two exited the west door of the hotel and almost ran into Dale Bryant, an attorney, and Ira Ward, the ice man, and fled south to the alley. The bloody shirt contained keys to a vehicle, which was in the Lucas garage nearby and had damage from the recent accident. The Model A Ford coupe was found an hour after the shooting, and was registered to Ralph Caraway in Cherryvale, Kansas. [2]

The acting coroner, Deputy Sheriff L. S. Markel, viewed Colver's body at the Lahey and Martin Mortuary. He believed a bullet entered Colver's right side and traveled downward and exited his left groin. Another round entered the back of his neck behind

---

2. "Merle Colver Shot Down by Bandit Pair in Hotel Here," *The Wichita Eagle*, August 14, 1931.

his ear, and a third bullet tore through one of his thumbs. The powder burns indicated the shots were in close range.

The suspects took Colver's gun, a .45 caliber Smith and Wesson handgun with a four-inch barrel. The serial number was 44134.[3]

Police learned that J. A. Walker, from Fairview, Oklahoma, was the driver of the other vehicle that got into a wreck with the suspects the night before Colver's murder. He was shown a picture of Wilbur and identified him as being in the other vehicle at the time of the accident. J. F. Robinson, who lived at 5835 South Lawrence Avenue, arrived at the scene of the accident shortly after it occurred. He also identified Wilbur as one of the occupants of the other vehicle. Harold Seigel gave the two suspects, one of them Wilbur, a ride to the city and dropped them off at Wichita Hospital.

At approximately 1800 hours on Friday, August 14, 1931, Patrolman Ray Mitchell and Jack Myler, a former motorcycle patrolman, were searching for the suspects when they observed two men lying under a tree at Linwood Park near the canal. Myler spotted them first and the police car drove toward them.

Wilbur Underhill stood up and tried to draw his gun, but it fell to the ground. He attempted to pull out a second gun but was shot at by Myler, causing Wilbur to drop the second gun. Wilbur ran, and Myler chased him while shooting at him two more times. One of the bullets struck Wilbur in the shoulder near the neck while the other bullet missed. Frank Vance Underhill, Wilbur's nephew, who was injured in the earlier accident, surrendered to Mitchell without incident.[4]

Myler later wrote that it was his second shot at Wilbur from fifty yards away that struck him, almost causing him to fall to his knees.[5]

During the foot pursuit, Myler lost visual of Wilbur in the alley between Kansas Avenue and Hydraulic Avenue, north of Harry Street about mid-block. Believing he was hiding inside of a shed, Myler fired a shot through it. He then spotted Wilbur hiding in the weeds and arrested him. A Lahey and Martin ambulance transported Wilbur to Saint Francis Hospital for his gunshot wound. Frank was taken to the police station for an interrogation.[6]

---

3. "Merle Colver Shot Down by Bandit Pair in Hotel Here," *The Wichita Eagle*, August 14, 1931.

4. "Youth and Convict Nabbed as Slayers of Merle Colver," *The Wichita Eagle*, August 15, 1931.

5. "Officer Tells Vivid Story of Thugs' Capture," *The Wichita Eagle*, August 15, 1931.

6. "Youth and Convict Nabbed," *Wichita Eagle*.

A one-year-old child, John George Colliatie, was struck by Myler's stray bullet during the foot pursuit while John was in his mother's arms. The round entered John's right hand and passed through to his right side. He was rushed to Saint Francis Hospital in serious condition. His mother, Mrs. Peter Colliatie, of 1612 South Ellis Street, was not injured. Mrs. Colliatie, John, and Betty Joyce Colliatie, three years old at the time, were walking near Linwood Park when the shooting occurred.[7] John survived the incident.

Frank, with injuries and mercurochrome on his face from the car accident the night before, told Captain W. O. Lyle and Detective Joe Maness the story of how Patrolman Merle Colver was murdered.

While he and his uncle, Wilbur, were in their room at the Iris Hotel, Colver knocked on the door to their room and entered. Colver sat in a chair; Frank and Wilbur were mostly dressed for the day at that time. All three obtained cigarettes and Colver lit Frank's for him. Colver walked over to a bed that had not been slept in and searched under the pillow and mattress, finding no weapon. Frank and Wilbur had both slept in the other bed, according to Frank.

Colver walked over to a window and hit a window shade with his nightstick, causing it to roll up some. Wilbur shot Colver, and Colver turned toward Wilbur and struck him in the head with his nightstick. The two fought with each other, and two to three more shots were fired by Wilbur, causing Colver to fall to the floor with his head between the dresser and the bed. Wilbur yelled, "Let's get out of here!"[8] Upon leaving the room, Frank grabbed a package and Wilbur grabbed Colver's gun. Wilbur threw a shirt into an empty room as the two fled.

Frank said three women were looking at them as they came down the stairs. Wilbur told the women, "There's been an accident up there. Call the law."[9] According to Frank, he and his uncle used the alleys to head south to some railroad tracks (most likely the Wichita and Western Railroad tracks). They followed the tracks to the river and then went into the willows. They observed several police vehicles patrolling parallel with the river throughout the day, but they remained undetected. They walked to Linwood Park and were near it when Mitchell and Myler spotted them.

---

7. "Struck by Stray Bullets," *The Wichita Eagle*, August 15, 1931.

8. "Youth and Convict Nabbed as Slayers of Merle Colver," *The Wichita Eagle*, August 15, 1931.

9. "Youth and Convict Nabbed," *Wichita Eagle*.

After being transported to the hospital, Wilbur acted as if he was unconscious, a tactic that officers believed would lead to an escape attempt, as Wilbur had done before. The city's physician, Dr. R. E. Hobbs, examined Wilbur and determined the gunshot wound near his neck was superficial and consented to his transfer to the Sedgwick County Jail. Still playing possum, officers used a wheelchair to roll him outside. Once outside, they stood him up and made him walk to the police vehicle.

Initial attempts to interview Wilbur were unsuccessful, as he was unwilling to speak about the murder of Colver and avoided eye contact with investigators. However, the citizens of Wichita soon learned more about Wilbur after his capture.

During the night of December 25, 1926, Wilbur and Ike "Skeets" Atkins killed George Fee, a young man, in Okmulgee, Oklahoma during the robbery of a drugstore. Atkins was later captured in Missouri and, in the process of being returned to Okmulgee County, was shot and killed by Sheriff John Russell when Atkins tried to escape.

In February of 1927, while in Picher, Oklahoma, Wilbur killed Earl O'Neal, a mine worker, when Earl attempted to detain the wanted man. He was eventually arrested and brought back to Okmulgee, where he received a life sentence to be served at McAlester Penitentiary for the drugstore robbery and murder. Wilbur escaped from the prison on July 14, 1931.[10]

After faking sick for a short amount of time in the county jail, Wilbur Underhill eventually decided to tell his story of Colver's death on Saturday, August 15, 1931, at approximately 1140 hours.[11]

> Colver first searched the kid's bed. He didn't find anything. He then drew a cigaret [sic] and lighted it. The kid gave me one and the officer held the light. I thought for a while he was going to leave. Then he turned to search beneath my mattress. I knew that if he found the gun, he would take me to the station and my fingerprints would tell the little story – the little story which would send me back to McAlister prison for life. I just decided it was time to act.... I told him I would show him my money bag. I reached beneath the mattress. The policeman must have thought I was searching for the bag. Instead I drew the gun and fired. The bullet struck him in

---

10. "Youth and Convict Nabbed as Slayers of Merle Colver," *The Wichita Eagle*, August 15, 1931.

11. "Fear of Arrest Caused Murder of Wichita Cop, Killer Asserts," *The Wichita Eagle*, August 16, 1931.

the neck. He then turned and struck me with his club. I backed away and let him have it again. I don't know how many times I fired. As he fell, the kid ran. I started to run. As I stepped over him, his arm moved and he mumbled something. I thought he was reaching for his holster. I kicked his arm and took his gun.[12]

When Wilbur was asked why he did not shoot it out with Myler and Mitchell, the officers who later spotted him, he replied with the following:

I intended to fight it out and kill them both. I reached for my gun first. It caught in my shirt. A shell jammed in the magazine as it caught. I dropped it and reached for the other gun – the one I took from the dead cop. As I started to raise it to take aim, the cop fired. The bullet struck the muscle in my shoulder. For an instant my right arm was paralyzed. The gun dropped to the ground. I knew if I picked it up, he would kill me before I could get another shot. I turned and ran.[13]

Wilbur was sentenced to life in prison on Friday, September 4, 1931, after pleading guilty to murdering Colver. Frank was later acquitted and freed after a jury was convinced that Wilbur was the culprit. As Wilbur was serving his time at Lansing Penitentiary, he led a successful prison break involving ten other prisoners on Tuesday, May 30, 1933. The escape occurred during a baseball game.

With eight of the prisoners armed, they kidnapped Warden Prather, after wrapping a wire around his neck and taking his set of keys to a guard post. They climbed the guard post and kidnapped two guards. Using the three victims to screen their escape, everyone involved was eventually lowered to the ground. They stole multiple vehicles and took the victims with them. Later that night, the convicts released the warden and two guards near Welch, Oklahoma without a scratch. The day of the escape was supposed to be an

---

12. "Offers to Take Life Term," *The Wichita Eagle*, August 15, 1931.

13. "Offers," *Wichita Eagle*.

uneventful one for Prather, as his successor was taking over as warden on Wednesday morning.[14]

Wilbur maintained his freedom and committed several crimes until his capture in Shawnee, Oklahoma on Saturday, December 30, 1933, where he was shot multiple times by a large group of officers. The United States Bureau of Investigation decided to move Wilbur to McAlester Penitentiary, the same place he escaped from in 1931, after hearing rumors that fellow gang members were planning to free Wilbur. He died in the penitentiary at 2342 hours on Saturday, January 6, 1934.[15]

Patrolman Merle R. Colver grew up on a farm in Clearwater, Kansas. After graduating from Clearwater High School, he attended Southwestern College in Winfield, Kansas. He was hired by the Wichita Police Department on January 21, 1924. When Ike Walston was chief, Colver oversaw the auto-theft bureau as a detective. Before his murder, he became a patrolman again and was assigned the beat near Douglas Avenue and Main Street. He worked the early shift from 0700 hours to 1500 hours.

A few months before Colver's death, he became ill and was diagnosed with Bright's disease, a kidney disease now known as acute glomerulonephritis. Doctors told him that he should retire, but he refused, and Chief Wilson allowed him to keep working. Colver lived with his wife, Mae, his sixteen-year-old daughter, Bessie Mae Colver, and his eighteen-year-old son, Robert Colver, at 1916 West Mentor Street.[16]

Two days after Colver's murder, Manly Wade Wellman described Colver's character in an article in *The Wichita Eagle*. He wrote, "Often had he stood on the brink of death, but never had his heart turned cold nor his feet faltered as he looked into the abyss. He was a hard worker and a capable one, with a fine record as a performer of routine labors, but he could rise to dizzy heights of courage, could and did face the grimmest danger. At the last he went to death like the hero he was, a fitting candidate for that Valhalla reserved for the souls of those who die 'with their boots on' that lesser spirits might live in comfort and security."[17]

---

14. "Wilbur Underhill Escapes from Kansas Penitentiary," *Miner and Mechanic*, June 3, 1933.

15. "Underhill Dies After He's Moved to Oklahoma Pen," *Sunday American-Statesman*, January 7, 1934.

16. "Merle Colver, Hero of Porter Meeks Battle, Not Afraid of Death," *The Wichita Eagle*, August 14, 1931.

17. Manly Wellman, "Records of Past Show They Always 'Bury Their Dead,'" *The Wichita Eagle*, August 16, 1931.

PART THREE

FALLEN OFFICERS OF RECENT YEARS: DANGERS ARE NOT ALWAYS IN PLAIN SIGHT

19

Patrolman David A. Kenyon

Date: October 26, 1962
Day: Friday
Time: 0230 hours
Location: 945 North Rutan Street
Tour: Three years, seven months (1959-1962)
Age: Thirty
Race: White
Gender: Male
Marital Status: Married
Military Veteran: Yes - Army - Korean War
Children: Two - wife was pregnant
ID Number: C0282
Burial: Wakita Cemetery, Wakita, Grant County, Oklahoma
Cause: Gunfire
Weapon: .38 caliber handgun
Offender Status: Convicted of first-degree manslaughter
Offender Age: Thirty-eight
Offender Race: White
Offender Gender: Male
Chief of Police at the Time: Eugene M. Pond

Patrolman David A. Kenyon. Wichita Police Department.

Patrolman David A. Kenyon was shot and killed at approximately 0230 hours on Friday, October 26, 1962, at 945 North Rutan Street while responding to a domestic disturbance call.

Thirty-eight-year-old Floyd Blockyou fired a bullet from a .38 caliber revolver, striking Kenyon in the head and killing him instantly. Blockyou was a United States Post Office mail carrier. He was a former Wichita police reserve officer until 1958, and served as a police officer in Henryetta, Oklahoma before moving to Wichita.[1]

Thirty-two-year-old Ruby Blockyou, Floyd's wife, called in the disturbance from a neighbor's phone. Kenyon and Patrolman William Dando responded to the call. Ruby later informed detectives that Floyd arrived home late from a night of drinking alcohol. After arriving, the two began to argue and he threatened to hurt her. Fifteen-year-old Michael Meek, Floyd's stepson, was battered by Floyd.

Terrance Meek, Rocky Blockyou, Eugene Blockyou, Rodney Blockyou, and Tammy Blockyou, the couple's five other children, were awakened by the loud noise. Ruby escorted some of the children to the neighbor's residence and made the call to law en-

---

1. "Family Fight, Stray Bullet Bring Death," *The Evening Eagle and Beacon*, October 26, 1962.

forcement. After Dando and Kenyon arrived, they went back with Ruby to her residence to resolve the conflict.

Detectives learned from Dando that Ruby wanted Floyd to leave their residence for the night, but he refused to go. Ruby decided that she would leave with their children, but Floyd wanted Tammy, their two-year-old daughter, to be left at their residence with him. The conversation over the child sparked another argument. Ruby agreed to go with Kenyon to the police station to fill out paperwork against Floyd that would have resulted in his arrest. They departed in Kenyon's police vehicle while Dando remained with Floyd at the residence. The two men spoke with each other as they drank coffee.

Dando convinced Floyd that it would be much easier if Floyd left for the night. Floyd indicated that he would leave, which prompted Dando to call the station to speak with Captain Ralph Strickland. Strickland told Dando that Ruby was good with Floyd's decision and would not sign a complaint against him. She and Kenyon returned to the residence, where Floyd continued the conversation with her. Floyd eventually grabbed some of his property and walked out to his vehicle in the driveway.

Floyd waited in his vehicle for a few minutes, while Dando and Kenyon waited next to a police vehicle parked in the street in front of the residence of 945 North Rutan Street.

The officers confronted Floyd about not leaving, and Floyd told them he would sleep in his vehicle. The officers informed Floyd that was not the agreement, to which Floyd indicated he could not find the keys to his vehicle. The three men attempted to find the keys, first inside the vehicle and then inside the residence. Floyd accused Ruby of having the keys, but she denied having them. The four adults continued searching for the keys.

Floyd and Ruby again argued about who would leave the residence, and Ruby told Floyd that she would stay at the neighbor's residence. She gathered some belongings from her bedroom, and Floyd followed her and grabbed a revolver without anyone noticing. The officers remained in the living room.

Ruby and Floyd reentered the living room, and Ruby called the neighbors to inform them of her plans. Floyd held his right hand behind his back and stepped out from behind Ruby. He pointed the gun at Dando and said, "Now you guys get the hell out of here!"[2]

---

2. "Family Fight, Stray Bullet Bring Death," *The Evening Eagle and Beacon*, October 26, 1962.

The two officers stepped away from Floyd, and Kenyon opened the front door and started to move outside to the front porch. Ruby became scared and ran toward the front door, when Kenyon pushed her out onto the front porch. Dando lunged at Floyd, who fired a shot in the direction of the front door. As the two men struggled over the gun, Ruby saw Kenyon was shot in the forehead and ran to the neighbor's house and called the police.

Dando and Floyd were on the floor of the hallway as they struggled with each other over gaining control of the revolver. A second shot was fired, which grazed Floyd's right leg. As they fought in the hallway, Dando grabbed the barrel of the gun and ripped it out of Floyd's hand. The fight continued into the bathroom, and Dando delivered multiple punches to Floyd.

Not knowing of Kenyon's death, Dando called for his help multiple times. Dando was able to cuff Floyd to a water pipe. He then walked to the living room and saw Kenyon on the front porch. Dando called the police dispatcher for an ambulance and more officers, who arrived within minutes.

When more officers arrived, they found Floyd in the bathroom still handcuffed and struggling to free himself. An ambulance took him to Wesley Medical Center, accompanied by officers, to receive treatment for cuts to his face. Floyd was then transported to jail. Later in the morning, officers learned Floyd had been grazed by the second shot and transported him to Saint Francis Hospital for treatment.

Chief Eugene M. Pond responded to the scene, and Lieutenant Floyd Hannon supervised the homicide investigation. Police learned the bullet entered Kenyon's forehead, traveled through his head, struck the glass storm door, and ended up on the sidewalk across the street.

According to Detective Major Joe Klepper, Floyd refused to give a statement and would not admit ownership of the gun.

Floyd and Ruby had a history of domestic violence in Wichita going back to 1954, according to police records. Ruby filed a complaint against Floyd on July 5, 1954, after she said Floyd threatened to kill her. She had the charges dismissed later in court. Several other reports of domestic violence between the two of them followed.[3]

The preliminary hearing was held in the Court of Common Pleas on Wednesday, November 14, 1962. Judge Daniel Dwyer allowed Eugene Blockyou, Rocky Blockyou,

---

3. "Family Fight, Stray Bullet Bring Death," *The Evening Eagle and Beacon*, October 26, 1962.

Michael Meek, and Terry Meek to testify. Rocky heard Floyd exclaim, "I'm gonna kill your mother," on the morning of the incident. The children testified they were at a neighbor's house across the street when the shooting occurred. Tammy Blockyou was at the Blockyou residence when the shots were fired. The stepsons said their mom ran with Tammy in her arms and said, "Floyd has shot a policeman. Call for more help."[4]

Dando testified and said when Floyd pointed the gun at him, Ruby ran toward the door with Tammy in her arms and saw Kenyon push them out onto the porch. Dando looked at Floyd, who cocked the gun and moved it in the direction of the door. Dando lunged at Floyd, but before touching him, he heard the shot.[5]

The first-degree murder trial of Floyd Blockyou began in February of 1963. The trial experienced delays and difficulties for prosecutors and the defense. On Monday, February 18, 1963, the jury was hopelessly deadlocked in Judge Clement F. Clark's courtroom. The case was then set for the April term.[6]

The second trial took place in April 1963. During the trial, Dr. M. M. Tinterow, an anesthesiologist, administered sodium pentothal to Floyd at the county jail in attempt to help his memory and to allow him to answer questions with less difficulty. Floyd's defense attorney for both trials, Russell Shultz, requested the injection.

During the first trial, Floyd testified that he could not remember anything between the time he was at the tavern the night before the shooting until the time he awakened at the county jail. Dr. Tinterow testified during the second trial that the drug might help someone answer questions with less difficulty, but this might include non-facts as well.

On Friday, April 12, 1963, Floyd took the stand and testified that he could now recall the events of the shooting. He said the discharge of the gun was an accident caused when Dando made physical contact with him.[7] The jury ultimately found Floyd guilty of first-degree manslaughter, and he was sentenced to five to twenty-one years in Lansing Penitentiary by Judge James J. Noone.[8]

---

4. "Murder Case Hearing Opens," *The Wichita Eagle*, November 15, 1962.

5. "Murder Case," *Wichita Eagle*.

6. "Two Murder Cases Placed on Docket for April Term, *The Wichita Eagle*, February 22, 1963.

7. "Truth Serum Angle Injected," *The Evening Eagle and Beacon*, April 15, 1963.

8. "F. Blockyou Readied for Prison Term," *The Wichita Eagle*, April 30, 1963.

The Gold Wreath of Honor was awarded to Patrolman David A. Kenyon and Patrolman William Dando. Also, both were named officers of the month for October of 1962. This was the first time the Gold Wreath of Honor was awarded by the Wichita Police Department.[9] Chief Eugene Pond and Lt. Col. Leonard Fraipont presented the award to Dando on Wednesday, February 27, 1963, at a police officer luncheon at Wolf's Cafeteria.[10] The City Commission presented the Gold Wreath of Honor posthumously to Kenyon on Tuesday, April 30, 1963. The wreath was given to Kenyon's widow.[11]

Patrolman David A. Kenyon lived with his family at 3881 East Roseberry Street. He joined the Department on March 1, 1959. He was born in Enid, Oklahoma, served in the Korean War, and married his wife, Peggy Jean. They had two children at the time, and Peggy was pregnant.[12] She later delivered a healthy baby boy in Oklahoma.

---

9. "Highest Police Honor Planned," *The Wichita Eagle*, November 17, 1962.

10. "Gold Medal Presented Policeman," *The Evening Eagle and Beacon*, February 27, 1963.

11. "Dead Patrolman Will Get Honor Wreath Posthumously," *The Evening Eagle and Beacon*, April 26, 1963.

12. "Family Fight, Stray Bullet Bring Death," *The Evening Eagle and Beacon*, October 26, 1962.

20

Officer Paul N. Garofalo

Date: November 8, 1980
Day: Saturday
Time: 0345 hours
Location: 1000 East 9th Street
Tour: One year, five months (1979-1980)
Age: Twenty-four
Race: White
Gender: Male
Marital Status: Married
Military Veteran: Yes - Army
Children: One
Badge: C1055
Burial: Calvary Cemetery, Wichita, Sedgwick County, Kansas
Cause: Gunfire
Weapon: Winchester .20-gauge, pump action shotgun
Offender Status: Convicted of first-degree murder
Offender Age: Thirty
Offender Race: Black
Offender Gender: Male
Chief of Police at the Time: Richard LaMunyon

Officer Paul N. Garofalo. Wichita Police Department.

Police Officer Paul N. Garofalo was shot and killed in the 1000 block of East 9th Street on Saturday, November 8, 1980, at approximately 0345 hours.

Garofalo was in the driver's seat of a police vehicle, and his partner, Officer Randy S. Mullikin, was in the front passenger seat when the shots were fired. The first shot struck the back of Garofalo's head and left shoulder, and came from a .20-gauge, pump action shotgun. The second shot struck Garofalo, as well as Mullikin's left leg. Mullikin received treatment at Wesley Medical Center and was released after a short amount of time.[1]

The Chicken Shack, a late-night disco located at 1001 ½ East 9th Street at the time, was a popular hang-out spot for people who lived nearby. Garofalo parked parallel with the south curb line with the vehicle running and the headlights on in front of the business. They spoke to two females through the open front passenger window, and while doing so, a male snuck up from behind the car and along the driver's side. The driver's window

---

1. Susan Edgerley, "Wichita Cop Slain on Patrol; Partner Hurt," *The Wichita Eagle-Beacon*, November 9, 1980.

was also rolled down, and the suspect was next to it when he fired two shots. Mullikin heard the pump of the gun and the two shots but never saw the suspect.

Some witnesses indicated the suspect fled in front of the police vehicle, but his exact direction from there was unknown.

During the shots, Mullikin bent down and rolled out of his door, called for help on his radio, checked on his partner, and recovered the shotgun that was left on scene. The gun was later tested for latent prints. A citizen also called for police, and many officers arrived on scene quickly. They blocked off the area, spoke to several people and witnesses, and documented tag numbers to vehicles parked nearby.

Some officers, before the shooting, referred to the area between 9th Street to Murdock Avenue, and Washington Street to Ohio Avenue, as "Murderers' Row." The area contained multiple pool halls, bars, and taverns, and was considered by many people a dangerous place to be in. Between 1975 to 1980, twelve people died from shootings, stabbings, and fights in the two-block by two-block area.

The weekend before the murder, Garofalo, Mullikin, and two or three other officers wrote parking tickets near the Loafer's Lounge. The Loafer's Lounge was directly to the west of the Chicken Shack. Later, officers entered the lounge and, when they exited, discovered two police vehicles had been vandalized. The next Tuesday, officers raided the lounge. A few officers wrote parking tickets not long before Garofalo was killed near the Chicken Shack on the same night. Later in the morning, during the homicide investigation, police discovered ticket books and a helmet were stolen from a police vehicle.

During the investigation, detectives believed that Garofalo, specifically, was not set up, and the two women the officer spoke with did not know the shooting was going to take place.

The initial description received by officers of the suspect was that of a black male, 5'11 to 6'1, twenty-seven to thirty years old, 170 to 180 pounds, having a medium afro, a medium complexion, and a black coat.[2] Some witnesses provided a good description of the shooter, as they were familiar with him from being in the neighborhood, but did not or could not provide his name.

---

2. Susan Edgerley, "Wichita Cop Slain on Patrol; Partner Hurt," *The Wichita Eagle-Beacon*, November 9, 1980.

Detectives followed leads that led to the arrest of thirty-year-old Ivory L. Haislip on Sunday, November 10, 1980, at 0430 hours at his girlfriend's residence in the 1600 block of North Volutsia, a little over twenty-four hours after the murder.[3]

Detectives did not believe the murder was racially motivated. Assistant Sedgwick County District Attorney Paul Clark believed it was a senseless killing and that the motive would probably never be revealed. He described Haislip as a person who worked a variety of jobs, including one as a janitor at the VA hospital. Haislip had been recently evicted from his residence, so he was living at his girlfriend's residence on North Volutsia in northeast Wichita.

The interview with Haislip lasted approximately three-and-a-half hours, but he would not comment on Garofalo's murder. Detectives' probable cause was largely based on witnesses identifying photographs containing the suspect. The shotgun that Mullikin located revealed no usable latent prints.[4]

When Judge Robert C. Helsel told Haislip his charges, he responded with, "I am not the man."[5] He informed Helsel that he had been in Wichita for the past fourteen months, and that he was from Dayton, Ohio. His prior felony convictions included one for forgery in 1975 and another for carrying a concealed firearm in 1978. Haislip was arrested for aggravated battery against his brother in Wichita on February 24, 1980, but his brother did not want to pursue charges in the case, thus Haislip was released.[6]

On the morning of Wednesday, November 12, 1980, Captain Kerry Crisp, who was the commander of the Adam 1 team, and six to eight off-duty and former police officers cut up a log that had been near 9th Street and Washington Street for over twenty years and was the site of illegal gambling and drinking. Along with the log, they removed trash and broken furniture. Law enforcement had wanted to remove the log from the area for a long time.

Residents of the neighborhood became angry when an officer posted a sign on a telephone pole near 9th Street and Washington Street that read, "Improvements in this area underway courtesy of Paul Garofalo's Adam 1 brothers." Police removed the sign after an hour due to a complaint from a citizen. Crisp said the sign was a "symbolic gesture

---

3. Susan Edgerley, "Suspect Jailed in Shooting of Policeman," *The Wichita Eagle-Beacon*, November 10, 1980.

4. Edgerley, "Suspect Jailed."

5. Susan Edgerley, "'I Am Not the Man,' Accused Cop Killer Says," *The Wichita Eagle-Beacon*, November 11, 1980.

6. Edgerley, "'Not the Man.'"

from our officers to Baker 1 officers to let them know Paul is not forgotten. It was not intended to inflame any passions."[7]

Officer Randy S. Mullikin spoke with Susan Edgerley, a staff writer for *The Wichita Eagle-Beacon* at the time, about a week-and-a-half after the murder. He indicated that he and Garofalo would trade off driving when they rode with each other. Garofalo was the unlucky one to be driving that night.

The incident unfolded very quickly. Paul screamed after the first shot, and Mullikin saw the flash of the second shot. Getting out of the car was his automatic reaction.

> "It didn't take me a tenth of a second to realize what they were doing. They were out to kill cops. Right down in that area, it is only me against quite a few people. At that time, they are just as scared as anyone else. Later they can help – and several of them did – but at the time no one knew what was happening."[8]

Mullikin fled the car for about thirty seconds to find cover and to see if anyone was coming for him. He returned to a roaring car because Garofalo's foot was on the accelerator. He pulled his partner out and started mouth-to-mouth. He told EMS when they arrived that Garofalo had a pulse. He learned later that his partner had died instantly.[9]

The preliminary hearing took place in December 1980. Nineteen-year-old Regina Franklin testified that she was talking with Garofalo and Mullikin in front of the Chicken Shack when she observed a male with a shotgun walk up and shoot the officer. She identified Ivory Haislip as the suspect. She stood near the passenger side of the vehicle when the incident unfolded.

Dale Jackson, who worked at the Chicken Shack at the time, testified that he saw a person who was talking with Garofalo on the driver's side of the vehicle. He saw a person approaching the police vehicle from the rear, heard a shot, and saw Haislip standing by the car. Jackson was unsure where the person who was talking with Garofalo went. Steve

---

7. Susan Edgerley, "Cops' 'Improvements' are Not Appreciated," *The Wichita Eagle-Beacon*, November 13, 1980.

8. Susan Edgerley, "Garofalo's Partner: 'I Think About Him All the Time,'" *The Wichita Eagle-Beacon*, November 19, 1980.

9. Edgerley, "Garofalo's Partner."

Islas, Haislip's defense attorney, pointed out inconsistencies between the two testimonies during cross-examination.[10]

Hubert Jeffries, a city sewer maintenance worker at the time, testified on December 10, 1980, during the preliminary hearing, that during the afternoon of November 8, 1980, he overhead Haislip say that he killed Garofalo. Jeffries had known Haislip for about three years prior to the murder.

Jeffries was at his girlfriend's residence when Haislip arrived with the nephew of Jeffries' girlfriend. Haislip, according to Jeffries, said, "I did it." When asked what he was talking about, Haislip explained, "I killed that cop."[11] Jeffries testified that he did not believe him. Haislip shook Jeffries hand before he left, and said, "Don't worry about me, I'll be all right." Sedgwick County District Court Associate Judge Elliott Fry bounded Haislip over for trial.[12]

On Christmas Eve of 1980, Haislip pleaded not guilty to charges of first-degree murder and aggravated battery.[13] The trial was delayed until May of 1981.

Mullikin testified that he saw Haislip a few minutes before the shooting not far from the scene, and Haislip did not respond when the officers greeted him. The officers started to leave and turned their car around, but they stopped in front of the Chicken Shack. The officers called Regina Franklin and Crystal Butler over to their car to talk with them. The shooting occurred shortly after that.[14]

Mullikin's testimony had some differences than Dale Jackson's testimony. However, the two accounts had a lot of similarities as well. They both testified that when Mullikin went back to the police car after the shooting, he and Jackson saw the shotgun to the west of the patrol car on the ground. The two men pulled Garofalo out of the vehicle and attempted resuscitation before the ambulance arrived. Detective Larry Warehime testified that the muzzle of the Winchester sawed-off shotgun was one to two feet from Garofalo when the suspect fired the shots.[15]

---

10. Lon Teter, "Witness Identifies Haislip as Killer," *The Wichita Eagle-Beacon*, December 10, 1980.

11. Lon Teter, "Haislip is Quoted: I Killed . . . Cop," *The Wichita Eagle-Beacon*, December 11, 1980.

12. Teter, "Haislip is Quoted."

13. "Haislip Pleads Not Guilty," *The Wichita Eagle-Beacon*, December 25, 1980.

14. Angelia Herrin, "Witnesses Say Haislip Shot Officer," *The Wichita Eagle-Beacon*, May 8, 1981.

15. Herrin, "Shot Officer."

Regina Franklin again identified Haislip as the man she saw shoot Garofalo. Assistant District Attorney Jim Puntch displayed a black jacket with beige piping, and Franklin indicated it was the same jacket that Haislip was wearing that night. Defense Attorney Steve Islas pointed out that Franklin described the black jacket as having a split in the back during the preliminary hearing. He had her raise the jacket during the jury trial, and it did not have a split. Islas spent a lot of time during cross-examinations focusing on discrepancies between state witnesses.[16]

Anthony Ray Martin was called to the stand during the trial and testified he saw a male drop a black pool cue case not far from the corner of 9th Street and Washington Street and walk toward the police vehicle. He said he thought it was a drug drop, so he went to the case to steal it. As he was leaning over to pick it up, he heard a shot, looked up, saw the muzzle flash from a second shot, and took off running and dropped the case. He identified Haislip as the shooter.

Before the shooting, Martin had been drinking alcohol, smoking drugs, partying, and riding around with a friend before going to the Chicken Shack. He said he grabbed a sandwich down the street. When he exited the door is when he saw Haislip, wearing a black jacket and carrying the case. He said he saw Haislip unzip the case, pull something out, and drop the case.

Martin testified the shots scared him, so he ran. After a few minutes, he returned to collect the case to rub off his fingerprints. Detectives from the lab testified that there were no usable prints from the case, but a fiber test indicated the case contained the sawed-off shotgun that was the murder weapon. Martin testified he did not talk to the police that day because he was scared.[17]

On Tuesday, May 12, 1981, the defense called Roslyn Parker to the stand. She said Haislip was "Not the man I saw with the shotgun. . . . That man (I saw) was Anthony Ray Martin. I'm positive. I know him and he know me."[18]

As she was waiting for a ride, she saw Martin walking with a sawed-off shotgun with white tube socks on his hands. She said they looked at each other when he walked by her. She said she knew something was going to happen. She observed him circling some

---

16. Angelia Herrin, "Witness: I Saw Haislip Kill Officer," *The Wichita Eagle-Beacon*, May 9, 1981.

17. Angelia Herrin, "3rd Witness Identifies Defendant as Slayer of Wichita Policeman," *The Wichita Eagle-Beacon*, May 12, 1981.

18. Angelia Herrin, "Witness: Haislip Accuser Was Real Assailant," *The Wichita Eagle-Beacon*, May 13, 1981.

parked vehicles and walk toward the police vehicle. Parker entered her relative's vehicle and heard two shots. She said she was afraid to go to the police because they could not protect her.

Following Parker, Reginald Woods testified that while in jail with Martin in February of 1981, Martin told him he "shot a police officer and stabbed another man, and 'shot two dudes with a shotgun.'"[19] The manager of the Chicken Shack, Nora Kemp, testified that Dale Jackson did not leave the business until after the shooting. Vicki Griffin, Haislip's girlfriend, testified Haislip was in bed with her and their young daughter when the murder occurred.[20]

The following day, Islas was scrambling and struggling to find more witnesses that would support the argument that Martin was the shooter, and not Haislip. Alice Glass, the aunt of Roslyn Parker, testified she picked up Parker before the shooting occurred, which contradicted Parker's testimony that she heard the shooting.[21]

On Friday, May 15, 1981, the jury found Haislip guilty of first-degree murder and aggravated battery.[22] On Tuesday, June 9, 1981, Haislip was sentenced to life in prison.[23] People claiming to be witnesses slowly trickled to law enforcement and indicated that Martin was the shooter, which prompted the Kansas Bureau of Investigation to reopen the Garofalo case in August of 1981.[24]

A Sedgwick County judge granted a new trial for Haislip in October of 1981 after two witnesses came forward.

A co-defendant trial was held in May of 1982 and the jury found both Martin and Haislip guilty, but the Supreme Court overturned the convictions "and ordered that Haislip and Martin be tried separately because each blamed the other. Haislip was convicted a third time in March 1984."[25]

---

19. Angelia Herrin, "Witness: Haislip Accuser Was Real Assailant," *The Wichita Eagle-Beacon*, May 13, 1981.

20. Herrin, "Real Assailant."

21. Angelia Herrin, "Search for Informants Slows Haislip's Trial," *The Wichita Eagle-Beacon*, May 14, 1981.

22. Angelia Herrin, "Haislip Convicted of Killing Garofalo," *The Wichita Eagle-Beacon*, May 16, 1981.

23. Ken Stephens, "Haislip Gets Life Term for Murder," *The Wichita Eagle-Beacon*, June 10, 1981.

24. Ken Stephens and Thomas Shine, "Garofalo Case is Reopened," *The Wichita Eagle-Beacon*, August 28, 1981.

25. Ellen Schechet, "Conviction of Haislip is Upheld," *The Wichita Eagle-Beacon*, June 22, 1985.

The prosecution believed that Martin supplied the shotgun to Haislip, who used it to kill Garofalo and shoot Mullikin. Martin was found not guilty during his second trial.[26] Haislip died in prison in 1999.

---

26. Ellen Schechet, "Conviction of Haislip is Upheld," *The Wichita Eagle-Beacon*, June 22, 1985.

21

Officer Danny D. Laffey

Date: January 5, 1982
Day: Tuesday
Time: 2322 hours
Location: 3100 East 13th Street
Tour: Three years, three months (1978-1982)
Age: Twenty-nine
Race: White
Gender: Male
Marital Status: Married
Military Veteran: Yes - Army - Vietnam War
Children: Wife was pregnant
Badge: C1021
Burial: Pleasant Valley Cemetery, Bentley, Sedgwick County, Kansas
Cause: Struck by vehicle
Weapon: Not applicable
Offender Status: Convicted of involuntary manslaughter
Offender Age: Eighteen
Offender Race: Black
Offender Gender: Male
Chief of Police at the Time: Richard LaMunyon

Officer Danny D. Laffey. Wichita Police Department.

Police Officer Danny D. Laffey was struck by a speeding car and killed on Tuesday, January 5, 1982, at 2322 hours on 13th Street near Lorraine Avenue.[1]

Louis A. Beans, eighteen years old at the time, was charged with involuntary manslaughter the following day in Sedgwick County District Court. According to Major Earl Wathen, a breath test showed alcohol had been consumed by Beans, but the "alcohol content in his blood was lower than that required for him to be considered intoxicated under the law."[2]

Captain Floyd Powell, Wathen, and Chief Richard LaMunyon described the series of events that took place: At 2311 hours, an unknown person called dispatchers and informed them of a fight taking place in the parking lot of the Zanzibar, which was a

---

1. Angelia Herrin, "Laffey Had Four Days Left on Beat 'Where the Action Is,'" *The Wichita Eagle-Beacon*, January 7, 1982.

2. Bill Hirschman, "Wichitan, 18, Held After Car Hits Policeman Checking Fight," *The Wichita Eagle-Beacon*, January 7, 1982.

nightclub located at 3105 East 13th Street, and weapons were possibly involved. Laffey, along with Officer Max Tenbrook and Officer Richard Witthuhn, who were in another police vehicle, were dispatched at 2314 hours.

The two police vehicles pulled into the parking lot of the nightclub at 2320 hours. The officers observed a black two-door sedan, occupied by twenty-five-year-old Alfred Yates, the driver, and his sister, the front passenger, back up onto 13th Street from the parking lot. The officers were on foot and stopped the car, which was facing to the southeast in both eastbound lanes of traffic. Laffey contacted Yates' sister on the passenger side, while another officer had Alfred step out to talk about the disturbance.

A green sedan, traveling east at a "very excessive rate of speed" in the inside lane, swerved into the outside lane just east of Lorraine Avenue and crashed into Alfred's car and Laffey.[3] To the west of the point-of-impact were 110 feet of skid marks. Laffey was carried with the car for sixty feet until it struck an abutment near the south curb line, throwing Laffey approximately forty feet from the vehicle. After striking the abutment, Beans' car traveled approximately forty more feet as well.

Beans was taken into custody. Alfred sustained an injury to his eye from flying glass and was taken to Wesley Medical Center. His sister ran from the scene. Laffey, who sustained major head injuries and internal injuries, was transported to Wesley Medical Center, and declared dead at 2355 hours. An autopsy revealed his spine was severed and had likely died instantly.

After Beans gave a statement to detectives, they believed the incident was unintentional, but LaMunyon said Beans drove with "wanton disregard for safety."[4] His driver's license required him to wear eyeglasses, which were not on at the time of the accident. He admitted his car was in poor shape before the crash, but the headlights on his car were working. The accident was not connected to the disturbance.[5]

Beans was convicted by a jury for involuntary manslaughter on Friday, May 21, 1982. The prosecutors' main arguments were that Beans was traveling fifty-five miles per hour in a thirty-five miles per hour zone when the accident occurred. His car needed repairs and should not have been on the road, and he was not wearing eyeglasses that his

---

3. Bill Hirschman, "Wichitan, 18, Held After Car Hits Policeman Checking Fight," *The Wichita Eagle-Beacon*, January 7, 1982.

4. Hirschman, "Car Hits Policeman."

5. Hirschman, "Car Hits Policeman."

driver's license required.⁶ Judge Nicholas Klein sentenced Beans to two years of probation on Friday, June 18, 1982.⁷

When Officer Danny D. Laffey joined the Department, he asked to be assigned to the Baker 1 team "because 'that was where the action is,' he said."⁸ A month before the accident, he asked to switch to days because his wife, Nancy, was pregnant with their first child. The request was approved, but the accident occurred four days before his new assignment started.

When Laffey returned from Vietnam, he briefly worked for the Wichita Water Department, then joined the Sedgwick County Sheriff's Office. He left there in 1975 to work at KG&E as a power-plant operator. He rejoined the water department, then was hired by the Wichita Police Department in 1978.

"He was real proud the day he came out of police academy [sic]. Seemed real proud of his work. He intended to stay with it. That was his life," said his father, John Laffey.⁹

---

6. "Man Guilty in Death of Officer," *The Wichita Eagle-Beacon*, May 22, 1982.

7. "Driver is Put on Probation," *The Wichita Eagle-Beacon*, June 19, 1982.

8. Angelia Herrin, "Laffey Had Four Days Left on Beat 'Where the Action is,'" *The Wichita Eagle-Beacon*, January 7, 1982.

9. Herrin, "Four Days Left."

22

Lieutenant John E. Galvin

Date: November 4, 2000
Day: Incident occurred on Friday - Died on Saturday
Time: Incident occurred at 1150 hours
Location: Incident occurred near 49th Street and Hoover Road - Died at Saint Francis Hospital
Tour: Twenty years (1980-2000)
Age: Forty-nine
Race: White
Gender: Male
Marital Status: Married
Military Veteran: No
Children: Four
Badge: C1096
Burial: Calvary Cemetery, Wichita, Sedgwick County, Kansas
Cause: Explosion
Weapon: Not applicable
Offender Status: Not applicable
Offender Age: Not applicable
Offender Race: Not applicable
Offender Gender: Not applicable
Chief of Police at the Time: Norman Williams

Lieutenant John E. Galvin. Wichita Police Department.

Lieutenant John "Jack" Galvin died on Saturday, November 4, 2000, from burns that he sustained from a training accident that occurred on Friday, October 20, 2000. He suffered from second and third degree burns over eighty percent of his body. He was a twenty-year veteran of the Wichita Police Department.

A firework company, called Western Enterprises, brought forty cases of fireworks, approximately 1,500 pounds, from Carrier, Oklahoma to the Wichita Police Department's bomb range, near 49th Street and Hoover Road at the time. The company wanted the fireworks destroyed and disposed of.

Some of the commercial fireworks were in the bed of a truck, and officers were in the process of placing them into two pits. Three explosions occurred with little to no warning.[1] The west pit, which Galvin was preparing, exploded first. The fireworks in the bed of the truck exploded next, followed by the east pit that was about fifteen to twenty feet away from Galvin's pit.[2]

---

1. Novelda Sommers, "Policeman Succumbs to Injuries," *The Wichita Eagle*, November 5, 2000.

2. Deb Gruver, "Explosions Burn Two Policeman," *The Wichita Eagle*, October 21, 2000.

Galvin was transported to Via Christi Regional Medical Center – Saint Francis Campus. He died about two weeks later. Thirty-nine-year-old Sergeant Douglas Manning and Christopher Sells, a city parks worker who was operating a backhoe, were also injured in the accident and taken to Saint Francis Hospital.[3]

About a year later, more details were shared by Manning. He had been in the Department for eighteen years at the time, and the training accident cut his law enforcement career short. The day of the accident, Manning was working in the east pit when the three explosions occurred. "First . . . Manning heard a sizzle. Then he saw a flash of blue flame, and he was knocked off his feet."[4] During the explosions, Manning caught on fire and suffered burns to his torso, head, arms, and legs.

ATF investigators believe the hot ember that sparked the explosion came from an earlier detonation in Galvin's pit. A safety procedure that existed at the time recommended that new pits be used for each detonation, or to wait twenty-four hours between blasts in the same pit.[5] An official close to the investigation indicated the bomb unit was most likely limited in space and could not dig new pits for each detonation. Approximately one thousand pounds of fireworks remained when the accident unfolded.[6]

Lieutenant John "Jack" Galvin was married to his wife, Mary Galvin. He was the father of Kyle Galvin, Adam Galvin, Abbra Fowler, and Shane Galvin. The City of Wichita held a downtown holiday lighting ceremony and a fireworks show in honor of Galvin. Western Enterprises donated fireworks to the show. Mary Galvin and the Wichita Police Department approved of the ceremony because they knew Jack Galvin would have wanted the show to take place.

While in the Wichita Police Department, Galvin coordinated community events, such as the Wichita River Festival and various parades, and ensured citizens remained safe while enjoying themselves.[7]

---

3. Novelda Sommers, "Policeman Succumbs to Injuries," *The Wichita Eagle*, November 5, 2000.

4. Associated Press, "Explosion Victim on Painful, Slow Journey Back to Health," *The Salina Journal*, November 12, 2001.

5. Associated Press, "Explosion Victim."

6. "Report: Embers Ignited Fireworks," *The Salina Journal*, June 29, 2001.

7. Denise Neil, "City Plans Fireworks Show in Honor of Fallen Policeman," *The Wichita Eagle*, November 28, 2000.

23

Captain Clay M. Germany

Date: July 9, 2021
Day: Friday
Time: Overnight
Location: 455 N. Main Street
Tour: Twenty-seven years (1994-2021)
Age: Fifty-eight
Race: Black
Gender: Male
Marital Status: Married
Military Veteran: Yes - Navy
Children: Seven
Badge: C1658
Burial: Lakeview Cemetery and Mausoleum, Wichita, Sedgwick County, Kansas
Cause: COVID-19
Weapon: Not applicable
Offender Status: Not applicable
Offender Age: Not applicable
Offender Race: Not applicable
Offender Gender: Not applicable
Chief of Police at the Time: Gordon Ramsay

Captain Clay M. Germany. Wichita Police Department.

Captain Clay Germany died from medical complications associated with COVID-19 on Friday, July 9, 2021, after he had been infected with the virus several months prior.

At the time, he was the commander of the Property Crimes Bureau, and his office was located at City Hall at 455 North Main Street. Germany joined the Department in 1994, where he worked his way up through the ranks. He started out as an officer, and later served as a detective, sergeant, and lieutenant. He was promoted to the rank of captain in 2016.[1]

In October of 2020, Germany had contact with an individual who was later confirmed to have had COVID-19. Germany tested positive for COVID-19 on October 20, 2020. He suffered from respiratory-related issues until he died in July of 2021.[2]

Chief of Police Gordon Ramsay described Germany as "a visionary, a consummate team player, a dedicated professional, and an exceptional leader," whose "service to the

---

1. Amy Renee Leiker, "Kelly Orders Flags Lowered for WPD Captain Who Died of COVID-19," *The Wichita Eagle*, July 16, 2021.

2. "Clay M. Germany," Kansas Law Enforcement Memorial, July 9, 2021, https://kansaslawenforcementmemorial.kansas.gov/clay-m-germany .

Wichita community was demonstrated in his ability to establish partnerships and be an effective problem solver."[3]

Prior to joining the Department, Captain Clay M. Germany served in the United States Navy and as an officer for the Midwest City Police Department in Oklahoma.

---

3. Amy Renee Leiker, "Police Captain Dies from COVID-19 Complications, Chief Says," *The Wichita Eagle*, July 13, 2021.

Categorical Data and Historical Analysis

Historical analysis is beneficial to police officers and citizens in several ways. We become aware of past environmental processes and how they evolved over time. Historical analysis allows for the development of critical thinking skills by teaching practitioners to recognize various associations, to explore different perceptions and perspectives, and to evaluate information from multiple angles to make good decisions.

By understanding the context of past line of duty deaths, we can fix current problems to prevent officer deaths from occurring. It helps police executives make sound policy changes that will benefit society and the safety of their officers. Police officers, by studying and understanding past events that transpired in their city, can develop a sense of self, a sense of community, and understand their place in history.

Through utilizing historical analysis, officers can be better prepared to make good decisions to prevent future problems.

INTERPRETING THE TIMELINE

1888

The year 1888 was an unfortunate one for Wichita and its police department. Eighteen years after it was incorporated as a city, Wichita was like a modern-day teenager, full of potential but with little experience, a short memory, and a small number of past mistakes to learn from. The Wichita Police Department's policy book was undoubtably thin, if it was written at all.

The three officers killed in 1888 had been forgotten on multiple occasions by the residents of Wichita and members of the police department throughout the years, even recently.

According to an article written by Pliny Castanien, that was published in *The Wichita Eagle* in 1935, Chief O. W. Wilson asked the pioneers of Wichita to search their memories for fallen officers before 1915 because the Department's records showed nothing before Humphries' murder. After searching the records and unsuccessfully checking other sources, Wilson had to rely on public memory to learn about the officers killed in 1888. This was necessary to prepare for a police officer and firefighter memorial that was erected in McLean Park in 1935.[1]

Wichita experienced a boom bust in the 1880s. It experienced tremendous growth in the decade, hitting a high population in 1888 of approximately 40,000 inhabitants. However, it lost one-third of its population within just two years. In 1890, the Federal Census counted 23,853 residents of the city. Resentment toward eastern banks flooded the city's residents due to numerous empty and partially built houses and buildings throughout Wichita.[2]

Roger Williamson wrote in his book, *The Wichita Police Department: 1871 – 2000*, "In 1888 . . . with the economic downturn the city did not wish to highlight that it was backsliding and the Wichita press stopped publishing population figures for the city in that year. The construction of the city and county buildings were about the only bright spots for the city during this time period. The population, because of several years of poor crops and slowing construction, began a decline."[3]

The Metropolitan Police Law, passed in 1887 at the state level, created and mandated boards of police commissioners for several cities in Kansas, including Wichita. The Board of Police Commissioners in Wichita was led by prohibitionist Hiram Lewis, who set sights on saloons that were thriving along with the city. A great deal of debate regarding the Metropolitan Police Law and the Board of Police Commissioners existed until it was disbanded by Governor W. E. Stanley, a Wichitan, in 1898. According to the late Craig

---

1. Pliny Castanien, "Who Are the Police Heroes of Wichita's Past?" *The Wichita Eagle*, March 17, 1935.

2. R. M. Long, *Wichita Century: A Pictoral History of Wichita, Kansas 1870-1970* (Wichita: The Wichita Historical Museum Association, Inc., 1969), 81.

3. Roger E. Williamson, *Wichita Police Department: 1871-2000* (Wichita: Wichita Police Benefit Fund Association, 2001), 23.

Miner, who was a well-known Wichita historian, "All it succeeded in doing was creating anger at the state and apathy toward the city government while residents continued to drown in their sorrows."[4]

The men of the Wichita Police Department, along with the citizens they protected, endured hardships after the passing of the Metropolitan Police Law in 1887. While sources regarding the Department in the early years are extremely limited, invaluable newspaper articles show evidence of dysfunction and discord in 1888, which may have been a factor in the line of duty deaths.

James Cairns had served as city marshal from March of 1879 to July of 1887, and was viewed by many people as the best police officer in Kansas. After his removal, his predecessor, appointed by the Wichita police commissioners, was W. W. Haines. According to *The Wichita Globe*, nine-tenths of Wichitans felt that "their constitutional rights have been trampled upon by the self-righteous puritanical law-givers." Several officers refused to serve under reappointment by the commissioners.[5]

Haines' entrance as the leader of the new Metropolitan Police was not received well by the businessmen of Wichita or the officers of the old force. Following the footsteps of the deposed Jimmie Cairns was a very difficult task. A respected man of the community, who was not named in a *Wichita Beacon* article, felt that removing authority from the men who helped build Wichita and giving it to new officers would cause trouble. The initial roster of seventeen men who were chosen to serve was published on Wednesday, July 6, 1887, and included the names of five officers of the old force who refused to serve under the new leadership.[6]

During the early morning hours of Saturday, September 17, 1887, about two months after being appointed city marshal, Haines received a telegram from the sheriff at Caldwell who wanted him to go to the gravel train to arrest a suspected horse thief. Haines went there and spotted a young man matching the suspect's description and gave him orders to exit the train out of a specific door. The suspect exited a door on the opposite side of the train and fled on foot. Haines pursued him through some weeds along Kellogg Street, fired four shots to scare the young man, but one bullet entered his back. The

---

4. Craig Miner, *Wichita: The Magic City* (Wichita: Wichita-Sedgwick County Historical Museum Association, 1988), 87.

5. "The Police Commissioners, *The Wichita Globe*, July 9, 1887.

6. "The New Policemen," *The Wichita Beacon*, July 6, 1887.

shooting of A. H. Ford stirred up a lot of skepticism of Haines' abilities and character to be the city marshal of Wichita.[7]

One of Haines' most prominent critics appeared to be Assistant Attorney-General Hallowell, who wanted the Board of Police Commissioners to fire Haines for failing to close saloons in the city around the end of December and the first part of 1888. Haines was able to convince the board to keep him as the head of the police department for a little longer. He was in this position when the first officer on the Wichita Police Department, Patrolman Kerwin, was accidentally killed in March of 1888.[8] Not long after, he was removed by the board on Thursday, May 31, 1888, because the commissioners felt he was "too lenient on the 'joints.'"[9]

The creation of the McMahan's Patrol in July of 1888 to protect businesses in the heart of the city, giving them policing powers alongside the Metropolitan Police, suggests that many citizens were unsatisfied with the public services provided by the city before the Patrol was created.[10]

Demand at the time for McMahan's Patrol, who did the same job in the same location as the regular police, apparently outweighed the potential consequences that could arise with the two organizations working alongside each other.

One of the worst outcomes occurred just two months after its establishment with the murder of Patrolman Ebenhack. To make matters worse, less than a month later, the owner of McMahan's Patrol, Chief McMahan, allowed Thornton, Ebenhack's killer, to return to his work duties while he was out on bond. This was short-lived but still outraged the community.[11] Shortly after that, the Board of Police Commissioners revoked the commissions of McMahan's Patrol. McMahan's men were sworn in as deputy constables on October 25, 1888, and continued working for a few years within the city.[12]

1888 was a challenging year for the Wichita Police Department. It was a time when political tensions were enflamed by issues that people were passionate about, such

---

7. "Shot in the Back," *The Wichita Beacon*, September 21, 1887.

8. "Hallowell vs. Haines," *The Kansas City Times*, January 1, 1888.

9. "Chief M'Namara!" *The Wichita Beacon*, May 31, 1888.

10. "The McMahan Patrol," *The Wichita Eagle*, July 21, 1888.

11. "An Outrage," *The Wichita Daily Journal*, October 18, 1888.

12. "McMahan's Patrol," *The Wichita Beacon*, October 26, 1888.

as prohibition, and a new state law fundamentally changed the policing structure of Wichita.

A respected chief was forced out the previous year by a newly established Board of Police Commissioners, who appointed an untested, less experienced person to lead the Department. With the removal of Haines in May of 1888, the Department's leadership was unstable, and the citizens they protected were lacking faith in them. Thus, the creation of an additional police organization that worked alongside the Metropolitan Police, while brief, only made matters worse.

The unhealthy culture, unstable environment, and the lack of leadership was most likely a factor in at least one of the three line of duty deaths that occurred in 1888.

1915-1931

America in the early Twentieth Century did not have a systematic way of enforcing the law, and officers of the time were poorly paid, often politically appointed, and lacked proper training and equipment. Coordination and communication amongst local police departments were deficient or nonexistent, and political corruption, especially on the local level, was common. The number of federal criminal laws in the book was small and there were far less federal law enforcement agencies in existence at the time.

Even so, the country was changing quickly, the population was growing rapidly, and life began to move at a faster pace with new technological advancements. By 1908, inventions like the automobile, trains, the telephone, and the telegraph made America's vast borders seem much smaller.

Several years earlier, the industrialization of the United States had started. The country was a new world power and much wealthier in the early 1900's than it had been before. Wichita was one of more than 100 cities in the United States with a population over 50,000 by 1910 and continuing to grow. But as the cities grew, so did the crime rate.

Unbeknownst to many people at the time, towns and cities in the early part of the Twentieth Century were breeding grounds for future criminals. Wichita was no exception.[13]

---

13. "The Nation Calls, 1908-1923," Federal Bureau of Investigation, accessed November 11, 2024, https://www.fbi.gov/history/brief-history/the-nation-calls.

Henry Ford's Model T was mass produced, starting in 1908, and made available to people throughout the country, including gangsters and thugs. Automobiles became attractive commodities to criminals, ensuring quick getaways and allowing them to conduct their crime sprees relatively speedily.[14] Wichita felt the effects of increased automobile sales when they experienced a growing traffic problem in 1910, where forty-four drivers were arrested for "fast driving" and seventy-two people were cited for violating the "Auto Ordinance."

In an attempt to combat the traffic problem, the number of traffic ordinances increased to fifty-two in 1912. Things were very different back then. The speed limit between Gilbert Street to 13th Street, and Seneca Avenue to Hydraulic Avenue, was twelve miles per hour. Outside of these boundaries the speed limit was twenty miles per hour.[15]

In 1914, the Wichita Police Department took a hard stance with traffic violators, and officers were ordered to arrest motorists for "major" violations, such as speeding and failing to have headlights (kerosene lamps), instead of issuing them a summons.[16] Area newspapers reported in 1915 that "'regulation of traffic remains a joke,' and that during the rush hour between five and six p.m. traffic was 'a sight for the gods and a menace to men.'"[17] The traffic issue in Wichita continued to evolve throughout the 1910s and 1920s, and it became a priority of the police department to gain control of it. The use of "electric cops," as the citizens called them, also known as traffic signals, became common within the city during 1925.[18]

It is no surprise that three of the fifteen officers who died in the line of duty between 1915 and 1931 were killed in traffic accidents.

The gasoline engine was a relatively new invention, and when it was mass produced and made available to the population by various means, it was inevitable that problems arose, especially in populous cities. While the Department had good intentions of getting

---

14. "The Nation Calls, 1908-1923," Federal Bureau of Investigation, accessed November 11, 2024, https://www.fbi.gov/history/brief-history/the-nation-calls.

15. Jordan D. Jones, *The First Century: A History of the Wichita Police Department 1871 - 1979* (Wichita: Jostens, 1979), 25-26.

16. Jones, *First Century*, 27.

17. Roger E. Williamson, *Wichita Police Department: 1871-2000* (Wichita: Wichita Police Benefit Fund Association, 2001), 35.

18. Jones, *First Century*, 35.

the traffic problem under control, its training, policies, and safety measures were too slowly implemented. These factors, combined with the use of motorcycles for enforcement efforts, were a deadly combination.

Combatting the issues involving alcohol and drugs was another major priority for the Department between 1915 and 1931. The country became "dry" in 1920, but Kansas, a leader among the states regarding the issue of prohibition, banned the production and sale of alcohol between 1881 and 1948. Bootlegging was highly profitable during this time frame and was a means for gangs to make money. Political and economic factors created the perfect environment for the creation and spread of gangs, which was at an all-time high in the middle of the 1920s. A crime wave never seen before affected the entire nation, and consisted of bootlegging, drug trafficking, bank robbery, auto theft, and kidnapping. Law enforcement throughout America, including Wichita, was not prepared for the crash.[19]

The Kansas legislature passed a law in 1902 making it illegal to sell cocaine without the permission of a physician. Druggists estimated that forty ounces of cocaine were being sold every week in Wichita the same year. While arrest records in the city were low for cocaine, they were high for morphine and opium. Newspaper staff believed most drug arrests were charged under morphine because it was difficult for officers to know what drug the offenders used. A reporter wrote in 1908 that many drug users in Wichita were "medicine addicts" who accidentally became addicted from undergoing medical procedures.[20]

A drug maintenance program was created in 1913 that involved physicians giving small amounts of drugs to addicts at the police station in hopes of slowing down crimes committed by addicted suspects. During the same time, a large house in South Wichita, referred to as the "Dope Fiend Hospital," was a place where drug users could go to sober up. Federal laws were established in 1915 that placed restrictions on morphine and cocaine, prompting the city to establish additional drug ordinances throughout the 1920s, indicating there was a growing drug problem.[21]

---

19. "The FBI and the American Gangster, 1924-1938," Federal Bureau of Investigation, accessed November 11, 2024, https://www.fbi.gov/history/brief-history/the-fbi-and-the-american-gangster.

20. Craig Miner, *Wichita: The Magic City* (Wichita, Kansas: Wichita-Sedgwick County Historical Museum Association, 1988), 115.

21. Miner, *Magic City*, 115.

Of the fifteen officers killed in Wichita from 1915 to 1931, eight of the suspects were believed to have an association with the use of drugs or alcohol, whereas the suspects in five of the officers' murders were associated with some type of gang involvement.

It is impossible to argue that Wichita was unaffected by the ailments that the rest of the country suffered from during this period. For the "Roaring Twenties" was the deadliest decade for law enforcement in the United States.

1962-2021

Compared to other large cities in the United States, the Wichita Police Department has lost a relatively small number of police officers in recent years. This can be attributed to luck, good training, new technology, and improvements in the medical field.

Losing one officer is too many, but in today's world, line of duty deaths remains a reality. Significant improvements have been made regarding law enforcement practices throughout the world in recent decades, including officer safety techniques, smart policy changes, new tools and technology, new laws and standard operating procedures, and the implementation of field training programs, to name a few. However, as society and law enforcement has become wiser over time, criminals have adapted and become shrewder.

While the dangers to law enforcement in the 1920s were not always in plain sight, they have become harder for officers to see in recent times. Who would have thought that Floyd Blockyou, a military veteran and former reserve officer of the Wichita Police Department, a person who was having coffee with an officer just a half-an-hour before, would suddenly switch gears and shoot a police officer in the forehead, especially in 1962? We now know this is a distinct possibility, as we have seen more cases like this in recent years and know more about substance abuse, Post-Traumatic Stress Disorder, and mental illness.

The amount of time that Officer Paul N. Garofalo and Officer Randy S. Mulliken stopped in their vehicle to speak with two women was very short. Who would have thought a man with a hate for cops would have enough time to obtain a sawed-off shotgun, sneak up on their car, and shoot them both. But he did, and an incident like this will unfortunately occur again.

Officer Danny D. Laffey was investigating a disturbance with a weapon call, something he had probably done many times before. Who would have thought that a separate danger, something that was not on his mind at the time, would approach him so swiftly, he would not have enough time to react?

Like Laffey, Lieutenant John "Jack" Galvin had been doing a task that was not uncommon for him to do. He undoubtably enjoyed his job, helped teach those he worked with, and probably learned something new every day. That terrible day turned out to be different and was both unexpected and unlikely to happen. But it did, and everyone suffered as a result.

The one thing that we all must acknowledge is that we can learn from it, and we have. The fallen officers would have wanted us to.

Today, the world is the same, yet it is different. Like the case with Detective Charles E. Galloway, Captain Germany faced an invisible danger. But his enemy was a new virus, not an old bacterium. Germany knew the danger was nearby, but how could he have avoided it when it was invisible?

The best thing officers can do is to follow recommended safety practices. In today's world, officers must be chess players, not checkers players. They must think about future problems that can occur, and about dangers that are not in plain sight.

An important thing to remember is that officers today can die in similar circumstances to all the officers that died in the past. Obviously, the situation would not be the same, though could be comparable. It's certainly possible that officers could be fatally injured today from the unsafe handling of a firearm, or an on-going dispute between two people that work for different agencies could lead to a bad outcome, such as it did in 1888.

According to the National Law Enforcement Officers Memorial Fund website, the causes of law enforcement deaths in the United States between 2014 and 2023 were wide ranging and included officers who had died from being shot and one who died from electrocution. Other causes included aircraft accidents, automobile crashes, beatings, boating accidents, bomb-related incidents, being crushed, fire-related incidents, floodings, drownings, falls, horse-related incidents, job-related illnesses, COVID-19 related deaths, motorcycle crashes, poisonings, stabbings, strangulations, train accidents, and being struck by vehicles.

The cause that had the highest total within those ten years was COVID-19 related deaths, affecting 802 officers. Following that was job-related illnesses with 585 officers, shooting deaths totaled 541, automobile crashes at 292, and being struck by a vehicle accounted for 150 officers. However, in 2023, the officers killed by being shot surpassed COVID-19 related deaths and job-related illnesses.[22]

CRITICAL INCIDENT DAY OF THE WEEK

The critical incident day of the week, not necessarily the day of the week they died, that was most common among Wichita police line of duty deaths was Friday with five officers. This count excludes Captain Germany because it would be extremely difficult, if not impossible, to determine which day he became infected with the COVID-19 virus. The critical incidents that occurred on Sundays totaled four officers; with three on Mondays, four on Tuesdays, one on Wednesday, one on Thursday, and four on Saturdays. The counts were similar for every day of the week except Wednesdays and Thursdays.

CRITICAL INCIDENT TIME OF THE DAY

Six Wichita police officers killed in the line of duty faced their critical incidents in the early morning hours between 0000 hours and 0559 hours. Seven officers' critical incident times occurred during the morning hours between 0600 hours and 1159 hours, three officers occurred in the afternoon hours between 1200 hours and 1759 hours, and six officers in the evening and late evening hours between 1800 hours and 2359 hours.

These counts do not include Captain Germany's incident.

Twelve officers' critical incidents occurred during daylight while ten officers' critical incidents occurred when it was dark outside.

LOCATION OF CRITICAL INCIDENTS

It is no surprise most critical incidents took place near the core of the city, because all cities start small and expand outwards over time. Generally, officers have patrolled the core areas longer than the outer portions of the city.

The Wichita Police Department's current Field Services Division is divided into five bureaus: Patrol North, Patrol South, Patrol East, Patrol West, and the Central Bureau.

---

22. "Causes of Law Enforcement Deaths," National Law Enforcement Officers Memorial Fund, accessed November 12, 2024, https://nleomf.org/memorial/facts-figures/officer-fatality-data/causes-of-law-enforcement-deaths/.

The Central Bureau's primary function is the enforcement of traffic ordinances and investigating accidents throughout the city. Meaning, Central Bureau officers do not respond to calls for service in the same manner that others do working in the four other field bureaus, who respond to all law-enforcement related calls for service.

The structure and organization of the Department has changed and evolved over time, as all police agencies do. The critical incident locations are based on the Department's current field structure, and not necessarily the structure at the time of occurrence.

Ten officers' critical incidents unfolded in what the Department identifies today as its Patrol South Bureau. This is not surprising, considering the oldest parts of the city are in Patrol South. Eight critical incidents occurred in Patrol North, one in Patrol East, and one in Patrol West. Patrol East and Patrol West include most of the land that are the newer parts of Wichita.

These numbers do not include Captain Germany's incident. Lieutenant Pugh and Lieutenant Galvin's incidents occurred outside the city; therefore, they were not included.

TOUR OF DUTY

The average tour of duty for the twenty-three officers killed in the line of duty within the Wichita Police Department is 5.16 years. All three of the officers killed in 1888 had less than a year on the Department. Only three officers, Gilmore, Galvin, and Germany, had more than ten years on the Department.

AGE, RACE, AND GENDER

The average age of the twenty-three officers killed is thirty-eight years old. Twenty-one of them were white males, and two were black males. There have been no female officers killed in the line of duty on the Wichita Police Department as of December 2024.

CAUSE OF DEATHS

Most of the officers who died in the line of duty mentioned in this book, fourteen in total, were killed by intentional gunfire. Two officers were accidentally shot, one died from

COVID-19, one from a duty related illness, one from an explosion, two from motorcycle crashes, one was struck by a vehicle, and one from a vehicle pursuit.

OFFENDER AGE, RACE, AND GENDER

There were fifteen offenders between 1888 and 1982, some of their identities unknown, that caused the deaths of Wichita police officers. The ages of some of the known offenders at the time of the critical incidents are unknown.

Of the known offenders with known ages (eleven of them), the average age is 28.05 years old. Of the fifteen offenders, nine were white, three were black, and three were unknown. Of the known offenders, all of them were males.

In the case of Captain Griswold, the suspects were believed to be males, possibly white or Hispanic. Eddie Adams and members of his gang, all believed to be white males, were suspected in the death of Patrolman Al Young. While a murder conviction never occurred in Patrolman James Fitzpatrick's case, there was strong evidence against Frank Foster, a white male, who was convicted of a different murder in Iowa. The primary suspect in Detective Edward Hall's murder, Ed Smith, was a white male; a jury found him not guilty.

MONTHS OF THE YEAR

The deadliest month for these Wichita police officers was November with six deaths, followed by July with four deaths. January, June, and August each had two deaths, and the rest of the months of the year had one death.

INTENTIONAL SHOOTINGS

Officers being intentionally shot by another person have been the primary cause of death for Wichita police officers since the Department's inception. Sixty-one percent of the Wichita officers who were killed between the years of 1888 and 1980 died by bullets intentionally fired by suspects.

Two of the fourteen shootings occurred on Sundays, three on Mondays, three on Tuesdays, one on Wednesdays, none on Thursdays, three on Fridays, and two on Saturdays. Six of the shootings occurred in the early morning hours (0000 hours to 0559 hours), two in the morning hours (0600 hours to 1159 hours), two in the afternoon hours (1200 hours to 1759 hours), and four in the evening and late evening hours (1800 hours to 2359 hours). Six of the shootings occurred in today's Patrol North Bureau, eight occurred in today's Patrol South Bureau, and none occurred in today's Patrol East or Patrol West Bureaus.

The average tour of duty of the officers that died from intentional gunshot wounds during this time period was 3.18 years. The average age of the police officers was 36.71 years old. Thirteen of the fourteen officers were white, and one (Officer Harrison Brown) was black. All the officers were males.

Nine of the fourteen shooters were white, two were black, and three were unknown. However, of those three unknown cases (the cases of Griswold, Young, and Hall), there were white suspects who were never convicted or prosecuted. All the known shooters were males, and the average age of the shooters was 29.05 years old.

Case Analysis

It would be a remiss to ignore the valuable lessons that each case provides, something that commonly occurs in law enforcement communities when incidents result in tragic endings involving their own officers. One way to approach this difficult task is to think about what we believe the officer would tell us about the incident if he or she could. While this analysis is primarily based on experience and may have subjective components, it can be highly effective if done appropriately and in a reasonable manner, similar to after-action debriefings and reviews.

In the cases of Patrolman Kerwin and Patrolman Hartzell, the common gun safety practices that most people follow today were not followed in those incidents. Ensuring the firearms were pointed in a safe direction and were unloaded would have prevented both tragedies. Additionally, if possible, officers should do their best to be in control of firearms that are in the same room and structure as them, and limit access to weapons to law enforcement only.

In Patrolman Ebenhack's case, today's policies of using handcuffs and conducting thorough searches of a prisoner immediately after an arrest would have prevented his death. Handcuffing behind the back was not common practice, and lightweight, easy-to-use restraints were not readily available at the time. Handcuffs existed before 1888, but the modern-day swing through handcuffs patented by George Carney were not readily available to law enforcement through the Peerless Handcuff Company until 1914.[1]

According to Gerald W. Garner, former police chief of Fort Lupton, Colorado, who has over forty years of experience in law enforcement, there are fourteen fatal errors that officers commonly make, one of them being poor approach or positioning. "By

---

1. "Setting the Standard Since 1914," Peerless Handcuff Company, accessed December 1, 2024, https://www.peerless.net/about-us#.

approaching a call or contact carelessly, or by letting a suspect move himself into a position where he holds the officer at a tactical disadvantage, American peace officers are murdered on a routine basis. There are, of course, all sorts of ways to position yourself in a tactically bad location. Letting an offender get way too close is just one of them."[2]

Detective Humphries placed himself in a dangerous position that was close to an armed, intoxicated, and unhappy individual. The pressure of being cornered by the detective, as well as his clouded judgement, may have been what triggered Auda M. "Audie" Caplinger to shoot Humphries.

Dr. Kevin M. Gilmartin, a behavior scientist that specializes in law enforcement consultation and issues related to public safety, wrote that police officers, like all people, form their views, thoughts, and predictions from the events that they encounter every day.[3] In essence, we are a product of our own experiences.

After Detective Humphries was murdered, *The Wichita Beacon* wrote the following: "Old time policemen, who are familiar with the work of the department for many years past, tell of many gun plays by men who thought they were bad, but in most cases they obeyed the officers when ordered to put away their guns.... In a few cases, officers have risked their lives by taking guns away from drunken or desperate men, and several of them have been shot at, but this is the first deliberate killing of an officer in this city."[4] Humphries, like all police officers, was most likely the recipient of many police stories about incidents that occurred in the past. Humphries' own experiences and knowledge of past incidents most certainly shaped and molded his own mindset.

About a year before his murder, Humphries was fined by Judge Campbell, acting judge of the city court, for striking Art Brasier with a revolver while attempting to arrest him. The detective was reprimanded by the court, which caused other officers to be apprehensive in using their guns while making arrests.[5] The fear of losing one's livelihood for making a significant mistake or doing something wrong, especially when that person has a family, can have a significant impact on one's behavior. It is possible for past discipline to cause an officer to be overly cautious, which leads to putting himself

---

2. Gerald W. Garner, *Surviving the Street: Officer Safety and Survival Techniques* (Springfield: Charles C Thomas, 2005), 9.

3. Kevin M. Gilmartin, *Emotional Survival for Law Enforcement* (Tucson: E-S Press, 2002), 23.

4. "Gun Toting and Alcohol Blamed for the Shooting," *The Wichita Beacon*, February 24, 1915.

5. "A Bottle of Alcohol Taken Off Caplinger," *The Wichita Beacon*, February 24, 1915.

or herself in a deadly position. This may have been a factor in Detective Humphries' incident.

Captain Griswold, Patrolman Harrel, and Special Officer Cruse's response to their call for service was not out of the ordinary, even by today's standards. It is not uncommon for police officers today to clear a business or a residence by having an officer watch one door while additional officers go inside through another entrance of the building on a burglary call. At the Bump shoe store, it appeared that the officers did not know if the suspects were inside or left prior to their arrival. Regardless, time was on the officers' side in this incident, and surveillance would have been a wise choice.

There is power in numbers. For police agencies in larger cities, calling for more officers is generally not a significant issue, as is the case in Wichita. It generally takes two officers on opposing corners to watch the perimeter of a building, and timing can be a major factor in officer safety. It would be reasonable to think that after looking at the store for a short time, a person would most likely see some type of movement through the windows or at the doors. Maybe a change in lighting or reflections will occur, or loud sounds could ring out if something is knocked over inside.

Another fatal error that Gerald Garner discusses in his book, *Surviving the Street: Officer Safety and Survival Techniques*, is hurrying when the circumstances do not require speed. He wrote the following:

> Yes, it's possible that you will have to intervene to save a life the instant you arrive on a scene. But it is much more likely that you will have at least some time to gather information, plan a course of action and get help, if you need it. There is a place and time for speed, but very many field situations do not require an instantaneous response from you. Slowing things down, taking in the big picture and avoiding ill-advised or rash actions could save lives – yours included. Speed frequently does not make for the very best decisions. Don't rush if you do not have to do it.[6]

Patrolman Harrel indicated that he observed a nearby door to a bathroom swing almost shut upon entering the business. If an officer today encounters a situation like this,

---

6. Gerald W. Garner, *Surviving the Street: Officer Safety and Survival Techniques* (Springfield: Charles C Thomas, 2005), 10.

most officers will probably agree that there is no shame in backing out of the business and waiting for additional officers to arrive on scene. It could be that this was not a viable option, given their positions in relation to the doors and the suspect.

Flashlights are an invaluable tool for officers, especially those who work the night shift. They can also make an officer a target if a violent suspect is on the loose or feels cornered. According to Wesley L. Harris, who served twelve years with the Ruston Police Department in Louisiana, the "lead officer should be the only one with his flashlight on, and he should use the button that allows him to blink the light on and off rather than leave it on continuously. Should a burglar decide to shoot, he will probably aim for the light."[7] Even flashlights have come a long way in terms of reliability and illumination, and the ability of a flashlight to temporarily blind a person today is much greater than it was one hundred years ago. Today's officers need to be mindful of when and where to use these instrumental tools.

Searching a person or a room can be one of the more dangerous jobs of law enforcement, as seen in Detective Ballard and Patrolman Colver's cases. Many officers have been killed after they failed to discover dangerous weapons during a pat-down or search of a suspect or prisoner. Some officers, who have the legal right to protect themselves, recklessly disregard the pat-down or search altogether when the circumstances allow for it.

Every year, officers in the United States are killed after failing to pat down a suspect.

Garner's book also discusses poor searching techniques and failing to observe a suspect's hands, which is equally important. "By neglecting to keep the hands of a subject or subjects he has contacted constantly under visual observation, a law officer is setting himself up for attack. It is the subject's hands or what he puts in them that can do you the most damage. By failing to always remain aware of them you are inviting disaster."[8]

Oftentimes, multiple people are inside of a residence when a search warrant is executed. If a decision is made to search a residence, it is wise to make sure that everyone is separated and outside of the structure. If a person is to be searched, thoroughness and attentiveness is critical to one's safety and to the safety of others.

---

7. Wesley L. Harris, *Police Patrol* (Springfield: Charles C Thomas, 1989), 80.

8. Gerald W. Garner, *Surviving the Street: Officer Safety and Survival Techniques* (Springfield: Charles C Thomas, 2005), 8.

Every officer who has been doing this job for years has probably missed some type of evidence during a search of a person, whether it was drugs or something else. If an officer says they never have, they probably did and just are not aware. Missing drugs on a search is one thing, but missing a gun is another. Having a gun in your possession for self-protection while doing the job, which a couple of officers in the past incidents failed to do, is extremely necessary in America today.

Vigilance is needed if an officer has information that the suspects were drug users and in possession of weapons. The level of suspicion and prudence should be very high after an officer observes ammunition in a room along with strangers. A careful pat-down or search of a person, if probable cause exists, and removal from the place to be searched, is a good start to staying safe. Every situation is different, and a lot of factors come into play. Regardless of the factors, an officer should never turn their back to a potential suspect.

Patrolman Albert Young's incident is believed to have involved Eddie Adams or a suspect from his gang. We will never know exactly how it unfolded, but it does highlight the importance of police officers staying vigilant, even when they are off duty. Like Young's incident, Detective Hall's case is also a mystery, though it appears both incidents occurred quickly, and the officers were most likely ambushed.

The practice of following a vehicle to the police station that is loaded with unknown people who could be armed, like Patrolman Fitzpatrick's incident, is uncommon in today's procedures. But it is certainly possible that officers, who are not careful, still do it, especially if they are in a hurry. This tactic should be avoided.

When trying to arrest a known violent suspect, especially one with a history of possessing weapons, by muscling them into handcuffs after they display indicators of noncompliance from the start, can be deadly. Detective Hoffman's life was taken in this manner, and Patrolman Scudder's incident had similar circumstances.

Having adequate numbers in the vicinity, combined with good cover, distance, and firm commands can mean the difference between life and death. Having a takedown plan and good equipment (body armor, shields, vehicles, drones, less-lethal options, police dogs, radios, public address systems) readily available can increase the odds in the officers' favor. But having these resources nearby is not always possible during a fast-paced event.

Patrolman Brown and Patrolman Marshall were fatally wounded during events that unfolded rapidly and with limited access to resources. Such a scenario is still a very real challenge for law enforcement today.

Injuries to officers during the performance of their daily work duties are common. Detective Galloway's incident underscores the importance of cleaning and treating those injuries, even if they appear to be minor, as promptly as possible. Exposure to viruses, bacteria, and other hazardous materials is also a danger that officers routinely encounter but are not always immediately recognizable. COVID-19 at its onset was a unique challenge to first responders when its characteristics were not fully understood, and vaccines were not readily available. Many officers around the world died from the epidemic.

There was an obvious gap regarding technological advancements with the use of motorcycles in law enforcement and the proper implementation of training and safety equipment in the 1920s and 1930s in Wichita. The deaths of Patrolman Ogden, Sergeant Gilmore, and Lieutenant Pugh are all evidence that adequate training, standard operating procedures, education, policies, and appropriate equipment were not in practice or implemented at the time. While police motorcycle deaths still occur in the United States, the gap appears to be much smaller with rigorous and continuous training.

The cases involving Patrolman Ebenhack and Patrolman Kenyon included suspects with both law enforcement and military experience. These incidents highlight the need for officers to be especially cautious when dealing with people who have similar training and experience as them and who are highly emotional or under the influence of a substance.

The more recent line of duty deaths in Wichita, excluding the case of Captain Germany, shows us how quickly a tragic event can unfold. Location and positioning are important factors that should be considered by officers, as Officer Garofalo and Officer Laffey's cases make known. Officers need to develop a "what can go wrong, will go wrong" mindset.

Ambushes, like Garofalo and possibly Patrolman Young's case, can and do happen, and will unfortunately continue to happen. Lieutenant Galvin was participating in a task that he had done many times before, and with little warning something terrible occurred.

Operating in today's fast-paced, sophisticated environment is law enforcement's continuous challenge. The ability to adapt is key.

Conclusion

The purpose of this book is to honor the fallen by informing current officers and civilians to recognize and understand the dangerous situations that past Wichita police officers encountered and died from. By studying major events of a certain locale, stakeholders can prevent past mistakes and problems from occurring in the future. This is one of the primary reasons we study history.

The most significant events in the timeline of a police agency often involve the deaths of its members, and the main priority for all police departments should be officer safety and keeping officers alive and healthy to protect others. If officers are dying, are injured, or cannot function properly, how are they going to protect citizens? Knowing and honoring our past, however imperfect, can make our future better.

A common mistake that many police agencies make today is keeping an event quiet as much as possible, when they should be learning from it. It is true that ongoing investigations must be protected to ensure the integrity of the case. Revealing vital details publicly too early can provide opportunities for guilt-ridden suspects to prepare alibis, a solid defense, or influence victims and witnesses. But avoiding a topic or tragic incident simply because we are embarrassed, or we do not have the energy, or because we are afraid to offend the sensitive nature of others can result in lost opportunities to learn and grow.

Another purpose of this book is a matter of convenience, simplicity, and truth. A person can easily find a website that gives a paragraph or two about how a police officer died, but it often leaves out important details that could be beneficial to the reader. This book certainly does not cover every piece of important information for each officer. Instead, it aims to create a clearer interpretation of what unfolded and is hopefully a good start for deeper case studies.

When the research phase of this book first started, it was discovered that not many books with the same goal exist. However, Steven P. Olson and Robert P. Brown created an inspiring account, documenting line of duty deaths in Baltimore, in their book *Some*

Gave All: A History of Baltimore Police Officers Killed in the Line of Duty 1808 – 2007. Hopefully, more people will follow their lead.

Analysis and research into line of duty deaths causes a person to realize how inaccurate some sources can be and how stories and information can be skewed and distorted over time.

It also makes a person realize how imperfect police organizations were, how much they have grown over time in wisdom and efficiency, and how great they sacrificed to protect the citizens they served. By studying a department's past, officers and citizens will have a more prosperous future.

APPENDICES

Appendix A

Officers by Date

John W. Kerwin	March 23, 1888
Henry Ebenhack	September 24, 1888
S. A. Hartzell	December 14, 1888
William L. Humphries	February 23, 1915
Frank W. Griswold	May 23, 1915
William H. Ballard	July 20, 1920
Albert L. Young	November 5, 1921
James R. Fitzpatrick	November 21, 1921
Charles D. Hoffman	November 25, 1921
Charles E. Galloway	July 15, 1923
Robert C. Scudder	November 30, 1923
Harrison R. Brown	January 5, 1925
Edward W. Hall	April 10, 1925
Vernon E. Ogden	June 26, 1927
Joseph E. Marshall	August 29, 1927
Paul E. Gilmore	June 18, 1930
James O. Pugh	July 31, 1930
Merle R. Colver	August 14, 1931
David A. Kenyon	October 26, 1962
Paul N. Garofalo	November 8, 1980
Danny D. Laffey	January 5, 1982
John E. Galvin	November 4, 2000
Clay M. Germany	July 9, 2021

Appendix B

Calendar Index

Harrison R. Brown	January 5, 1925
Danny D. Laffey	January 5, 1982
William L. Humphries	February 23, 1915
John W. Kerwin	March 23, 1888
Edward W. Hall	April 10, 1925
Frank W. Griswold	May 23, 1915
Paul E. Gilmore	June 18, 1930
Vernon E. Ogden	June 26, 1927
Clay M. Germany	July 9, 2021
Charles E. Galloway	July 15, 1923
William H. Ballard	July 20, 1920
James O. Pugh	July 31, 1930
Merle R. Colver	August 14, 1931
Joseph E. Marshall	August 29, 1927
Henry Ebenhack	September 24, 1888
David A. Kenyon	October 26, 1962
John E. Galvin	November 4, 2000
Albert L. Young	November 5, 1921
Paul N. Garofalo	November 8, 1980
James R. Fitzpatrick	November 21, 1921
Charles D. Hoffman	November 25, 1921
Robert C. Scudder	November 30, 1923
S. A. Hartzell	December 14, 1888

Appendix C

Alphabetical Roll of Officers

Ballard, William H.
Brown, Harrison R.
Colver, Merle R.
Ebenhack, Henry
Fitzpatrick, James R.
Galloway, Charles E.
Galvin, John E.
Garofalo, Paul N.
Germany, Clay M.
Gilmore, Paul E.
Griswold, Frank W.
Hall, Edward W.
Hartzell, S. A.
Hoffman, Charles D.
Humphries, William L.
Kenyon, David A.
Kerwin, John W.
Laffey, Danny D.
Marshall, Joseph E.
Ogden, Vernon E.
Pugh, James O.
Scudder, Robert C.
Young, Albert L.

BIBLIOGRAPHY

American-Statesman. "Underhill Dies After He's Moved to Oklahoma Pen." January 7, 1934.

Arkansas City Daily Traveler. "Wichita Motor Cop Murdered Early Today." November 21, 1921.

Associated Press. "Explosion Victim on Painful, Slow Journey Back to Health." *The Salina Journal*. November 12, 2001.

The Coffeyville Daily Journal. November 8, 1921.

Edgerley, Susan. "Cops 'Improvements' are Not Appreciated." *The Wichita Eagle-Beacon*. November 13, 1980.

Edgerley, Susan. "Garofalo's Partner: 'I think About Him All the Time.'" *The Wichita Eagle-Beacon*. November 19, 1980.

Edgerley, Susan. "'I Am Not the Man,' Accused Cop Killer Says." *The Wichita Eagle-Beacon*. November 11, 1980.

Edgerley, Susan. "Suspect Jailed in Shooting of Policeman." *The Wichita Eagle-Beacon*. November 10, 1980.

Edgerley, Susan. "Wichita Cop Slain on Patrol; Partner Hurt." *The Wichita Eagle-Beacon*. November 9, 1980.

The Emporia Gazette. "Acquit Ex-Policeman." March 11, 1927.

The Emporia Gazette. "Foor's Case Goes to Jury Today." June 30, 1924.

The Emporia Gazette. "Foor's Victim Dies." November 30, 1923.

The Evening Eagle and Beacon. "Dead Patrolman Will Get Honor Wreath Posthumously." April 26, 1963.

The Evening Eagle and Beacon. "Family Fight, Stray Bullet Bring Death." October 26, 1962.

The Evening Eagle and Beacon. "Gold Medal Presented Policeman." February 27, 1963.

The Evening Eagle and Beacon. "Truth Serum Angle Injected." April 15, 1963.

Federal Bureau of Investigation. "The FBI and the American Gangster, 1924-1938." Accessed November 11, 2024. https://www.fbi.gov/history/brief-history/the-fbi-and-the-american-gangster.

Federal Bureau of Investigation. "The Nation Calls, 1908-1923." Accessed November 11, 2024. https://www.fbi.gov/history/brief-history/the-natin-calls.

Gagnon, Bill. "End of Gang Reign Cost 3 Lives Here." *The Wichita Eagle*. November 15, 1953.

Garner, Gerald W. *Surviving the Street: Officer Safety and Survival Techniques.* Springfield: Charles C. Thomas, 2005.

Gilmartin, Kevin M. *Emotional Survival for Law Enforcement.* Tucson: E-S Press, 2002.

Gruver, Deb. "Explosions Burn Two Policeman." *The Wichita Eagle*. October 21, 2000.

Harris, Wesley L. *Police Patrol.* Springfield: Charles C. Thomas, 1989.

Herrin, Angelia. "Haislip Convicted of Killing Garofalo." *The Wichita Eagle-Beacon*. May 16, 1981.

Herrin, Angelia. "Laffey Had Four Days Left on Beat 'Where the Action Is.'" *The Wichita Eagle-Beacon*. January 7, 1982.

Herrin, Angelia. "Search for Informants Slows Haislip's Trial." *The Wichita Eagle-Beacon*. May 14, 1981.

Herrin, Angelia. "3rd Witness Identifies Defendant as Slayer of Wichita Policeman." *The Wichita Eagle-Beacon*. May 12, 1981.

Herrin, Angelia. "Witnesses Say Haislip Shot Officer." *The Wichita Eagle-Beacon*. May 8, 1981.

Herrin, Angelia. "Witness: Haislip Accuser Was Real Assailant." *The Wichita Eagle-Beacon*. May 13, 1981.

Herrin, Angelia. "Witness: I Saw Haislip Kill Officer." *The Wichita Eagle-Beacon*. May 9, 1981.

Hirschman, Bill. "Wichitan, 18, Held After Car Hits Policeman Checking Fight." *The Wichita Eagle-Beacon*. January 7, 1982.

Jones, Jordan D. *The First Century: A History of the Wichita Police Department 1871-1979*. Wichita: Jostens, 1979.

The Kansas City Times. "Hallowell vs. Haines." January 1, 1888.

Kansas Law Enforcement Memorial. July 9, 2021. https://kansaslawenforcementmemorial.kansas.gov/clay-m-germany.

Kansas Masonic Digest. "Lieut. Jimmie Pugh Dies of Tetanus Following Injuries." August 1, 1930.

Leiker, Amy Renee. "Kelly Orders Flags Lowered for WPD Captain Who Died of COVID-19." *The Wichita Eagle.* July 16, 2021.

Leiker, Amy Renee. "Police Captain Dies from COVID-19 Complications, Chief Says." *The Wichita Eagle.* July 13, 2021.

The Manhattan Mercury. "Wichita Officer Slain by Bandits." August 27, 1927.

The Meade County News. "Mother Sues Druggist." March 18, 1915.

The Meade County News. "Obituary." June 1, 1911.

Measuring Worth. Accessed November 16, 2016. https://www.measuringworth.com/.

Miner and Mechanic. "Wilbur Underhill Escapes from Kansas Penitentiary." June 3, 1933.

The Mocking Bird. "Police Officer Hartzell, of Wichita, Accidentally Shot and Killed Last Thursday." December 22, 1888.

National Law Enforcement Officers Memorial Fund. "Causes of Law Enforcement Deaths." Accessed November 12, 2024. https://nleomf.org/memorial/facts-figures/officer-fatality-data/causes-of-law-enforcement-deaths/.

Neil, Denise. "City Plans Fireworks Show in Honor of Fallen Policeman." *The Wichita Eagle.* November 28, 2000.

The Negro Star. "Policeman Brown Killed." January 9, 1925.

Peerless Handcuff Company. "Setting the Standard Since 1914." Accessed December 1, 2024. https://www.peerless.net/about-us.

Price, Jay M. *Wichita: 1860-1930.* Charleston: Arcadia Publishing, 2003.

The Salina Journal. "Report: Embers Ignited Fireworks." June 29, 2001.

Schechet, Ellen. "Conviction of Haislip is Upheld." *The Wichita Eagle-Beacon.* June 22, 1985.

Sommers, Novelda. "Policeman Succumbs to Injuries." *The Wichita Eagle.* November 5, 2000.

Stephens, Ken, and Thomas Shine. "Garofalo Case is Reopened." *The Wichita Eagle-Beacon.* August 28, 1981.

Stephens, Ken. "Haislip Gets Life Term for Murder." *The Wichita Eagle-Beacon.* June 10, 1981.

The Sun. "Charles Bledsoe Not Guilty." February 18, 1921.

Tanner, Beccy. *Bear Grease, Builders and Bandits: The Men and Women of Wichita's Past*. Wichita: The Wichita Eagle and Beacon Publishing Company, 1991.

Tanner, Beccy. "Notorious Bandit Holds Colorful Spot in History." *The Wichita Eagle*. July 15, 1993.

Teter, Lon. "Haislip is Quoted: I Killed . . . Cop." *The Wichita Eagle-Beacon*. December 11, 1980.

Teter, Lon. "Witness Identifies Haislip as Killer." *The Wichita Eagle-Beacon*. December 10, 1980.

The Topeka Daily Capital. "Rewards for Wichita Slayers Exceed $3000." September 20, 1916.

U.S. Census Bureau. "Population of the 100 Largest Urban Places: 1920." Accessed October 27, 2016. https://www.census.gov/population/www/documentation/twps0027/tab15.txt.

The Wellington Daily News. "Murdered Policeman Formerly Live Here." November 9, 1921.

Wellman, Manly. "Records of Past Show They Always 'Bury Their Dead.'" *The Wichita Eagle*. August 16, 1931.

The Wichita Beacon. "Baird Confesses the Murder of Ballard." August 6, 1920.

The Wichita Beacon. "Baird is Guilty in First Degree." November 16, 1920.

The Wichita Beacon. "A Benefit." March 24, 1888.

The Wichita Beacon. "A Bottle of Alcohol Taken Off Caplinger." February 24, 1915.

The Wichita Beacon. "Burglars, Trapped in Store Slay Police Captain; Escape." May 24, 1915.

The Wichita Beacon. "Chapel Too Small for the Mourners." February 24, 1915.

The Wichita Beacon. "Charles Hoffman, Detective, Dies; Adams' Last Victim." November 25, 1921.

The Wichita Beacon. "Chief M'Namara!" May 31, 1888.

The Wichita Beacon. "Desperado Kills Officer Ballard and Wounds Two." July 21, 1920.

The Wichita Beacon. "Detectives Get Equal Credit for Killing Adams." November 30, 1921.

The Wichita Beacon. "Driver of Machine Involved in Fatal Accident Cleared." July 9, 1927.

The Wichita Beacon. "First Degree, Their Verdict." November 12, 1915.

BIBLIOGRAPHY

The Wichita Beacon. "Girls in Death Car Fear Killer of Fitzpatrick Will Slay Them." December 3, 1921.

The Wichita Beacon. "Gun Toting and Alcohol Blamed for the Shooting." February 24, 1915.

The Wichita Beacon. "Hoffman Did Not Recognize Adams, Stuckey Believes." November 22, 1921.

The Wichita Beacon. "Humphries Shot to Death While Making an Arrest." February 23, 1915.

The Wichita Beacon. "In the Crucible." June 27, 1927.

The Wichita Beacon. "McMahan's Patrol." July 16, 1888.

The Wichita Beacon. "McMahan's Patrol." October 26, 1888.

The Wichita Beacon. "Most Popular Officer Dies." June 18, 1930.

The Wichita Beacon. "Motorcycle Officer Laid to Rest." June 28, 1927.

The Wichita Beacon. "A Murder or Manslaughter." November 10, 1915.

The Wichita Beacon. "Officer Think Baird Bad Actor." November 20, 1920.

The Wichita Beacon. "Policeman's *[sic]* Kerwin's Funeral." March 24, 1888.

The Wichita Beacon. "Police in Mourning for the Dead Officer." February 24, 1915.

The Wichita Beacon. "Released on Bond." October 4, 1888.

The Wichita Beacon. "Shot Rambo First and then Ballard." August 9, 1920.

The Wichita Beacon. "Signal at Fatal Crossing Working, Says Investigator." June 30, 1927.

The Wichita Beacon. "3 Shot by Gunmen Today." November 21, 1921.

The Wichita Beacon. "Through the Heart." March 23, 1888.

The Wichita Daily Journal. "An Outrage." October 18, 1888.

The Wichita Eagle. "Accidentally Shot Scudder Foor Asserts." December 3, 1923.

The Wichita Eagle. "Accused Killer of E. W. Hall on Way to Wichita." July 20, 1926.

The Wichita Eagle. "Admits the Shooting of Wichita Policeman but Reason Unknown." November 30, 1923.

The Wichita Eagle. "Arraign Foor as Soon as He Can Leave Hospital." December 4, 1923.

The Wichita Eagle. "Arrest 2 Men as Suspects in the Slaying of Hall." April 11, 1925.

The Wichita Eagle. "Bandit Killer's Wish for Larger Gun to be Realized Today in a New $50 Pistol." September 1, 1927.

The Wichita Eagle-Beacon. "Driver is Put on Probation." June 19, 1982.

The Wichita Eagle-Beacon. "Haislip Pleads Not Guilty." December 25, 1980.

The Wichita Eagle-Beacon. "Man Guilty in Death of Officer." May 22, 1982.

The Wichita Eagle. "Believed Her Husband Would be Safe on Down-town Beat." December 1, 1923.

The Wichita Eagle. "Benefit Dance at the Ritz for Officer Hurt in Line of Duty Here." October 3, 1929.

The Wichita Eagle. "Bitter Fight is Being Waged for a Stallcup Jury." November 1, 1927.

The Wichita Eagle. "Blood Poisoning Fatal to Charles Galloway Today." July 15, 1923.

The Wichita Eagle. "Burnside Passes Just Year After Companion Slain." April 9, 1926.

The Wichita Eagle. "Citizens Discuss Murders." October 19, 1915.

The Wichita Eagle. "Confesses for Dope." October 23, 1921.

The Wichita Eagle. "Cop Chasing Speeder Hurt." September 21, 1929.

The Wichita Eagle. "Cop Claims Title 'Hard Luck Champ.'" May 6, 1930.

The Wichita Eagle. "The Coroner's Verdict." September 26, 1888.

The Wichita Eagle. "Crippled Cop Unaware of Loss." July 21, 1930.

The Wichita Eagle. "Death in Hunch of a Woman." September 1, 1927.

The Wichita Eagle. "Detective Hall Killed in Battle with Two Bandits." April 10, 1925.

The Wichita Eagle. "Fatal Accident." December 14, 1888.

The Wichita Eagle. "F. Blockyou Readied for Prison Term." April 30, 1963.

The Wichita Eagle. "Fear of Arrest Caused Murder of Wichita Cop, Killer Asserts." August 16, 1931.

The Wichita Eagle. "First Reward for Detective Slayer Offered Tuesday." April 15, 1925.

The Wichita Eagle. "Foor Fired Shot Killing Scudder is Jury's Report." December 6, 1923.

The Wichita Eagle. "Foor Shot Self During Gun Fight, Officers Testify." June 27, 1924.

The Wichita Eagle. "4 Hours Without Verdict." December 11, 1926.

The Wichita Eagle. "Fugitive Bandit Eludes Police Net." August 29, 1927.

The Wichita Eagle. "Galloway Seriously Ill." July 11, 1923.

The Wichita Eagle. "Gets Little Sleep." April 17, 1925.

The Wichita Eagle. "Guard is Placed at Bedside of Man who Murdered Scudder." December 1, 1923.

The Wichita Eagle. "Gunman Kills One and Wounds Two Policeman." July 21, 1920.

The Wichita Eagle. "Hard Luck Dogs Cop." June 14, 1930.

The Wichita Eagle. "Highest Police Honor Planned." November 17, 1962.

The Wichita Eagle. "Holding Wounded Man." April 18, 1925.

The Wichita Eagle. "Hold Ray H. Foor Responsible for Scudder's Death." July 2, 1924.

The Wichita Eagle. "Injured Officer in Bad Condition." July 26, 1930.

The Wichita Eagle. "The Inquest." December 15, 1888.

The Wichita Eagle. "Jury is Chosen; Baird Hearing Set for Monday." November 13, 1920.

The Wichita Eagle. "Kelley Gets 40 Years." March 10, 1925.

The Wichita Eagle. "Kill Adams and Rout Gang." November 23, 1921.

The Wichita Eagle. "Kills Detective Who Tries to Arrest Him." February 24, 1915.

The Wichita Eagle. "Law and Order has Lost One of Its Best Friends." July 16, 1923.

The Wichita Eagle. "Lieut. Jimmie Pugh Loses Right Leg in Crash Near Wichita." July 21, 1930.

The Wichita Eagle. "Lose Hope as Lockjaw Hits Jimmy Pugh." July 31, 1930.

The Wichita Eagle. "Many Speculate about Shooting." November 7, 1921.

The Wichita Eagle. "The McMahan Patrol." July 21, 1888.

The Wichita Eagle. "Merle Colver, Hero of Porter Meeks Battle, Not Afraid of Death." August 14, 1931.

The Wichita Eagle. "Merle Colver Shot Down by Bandit Pair in Hotel Here." August 14, 1931.

The Wichita Eagle. "Mile-long Procession." June 29, 1927.

The Wichita Eagle. "Miss Averill Gay." March 15, 1926.

The Wichita Eagle. "Murder Case Hearing Opens." November 15, 1962.

The Wichita Eagle. "Negro Policeman Shot Here Sunday May Not Recover." January 5, 1925.

The Wichita Eagle. "New Court Record Set as Ossweiler Verdict Returned." November 28, 1927.

The Wichita Eagle. "Not Sure Burglars Mexicans." May 25, 1915.

The Wichita Eagle. "Offers to Take Life Term." August 15, 1931.

The Wichita Eagle. "Officer's Widow Dies." June 28, 1925.

The Wichita Eagle. "Officer Tells Vivid Story of Thugs' Capture." August 15, 1931.

The Wichita Eagle. "Patrolman Dies After Assailant Admits Shooting." January 6, 1925.

The Wichita Eagle. "Probe Report of Threatening Note." November 9, 1921.

The Wichita Eagle. "Pugh Still in Danger." July 23, 1930.

The Wichita Eagle. "Robert Scudder Buried Monday." December 4, 1923.

The Wichita Eagle. "Scudder Death Inquest is Set for Wednesday." December 2, 1923.

The Wichita Eagle. "Sealed Verdict is Returned in Ed Smith Trial." March 11, 1927.

The Wichita Eagle. "Seek the Woman." November 13, 1921.

The Wichita Eagle. "Selling of Liquor Costs Davis $500." June 30, 1917.

The Wichita Eagle. "Shot Dead." September 25, 1888.

The Wichita Eagle. "Slayer Changes Plea, Deciding to Stand Trial." January 7, 1925.

The Wichita Eagle. "State Vs. Thornton." April 10, 1889.

The Wichita Eagle. "State Vs. Thornton." January 10, 1889.

The Wichita Eagle. "Struck by Stray Bullets." August 15, 1931.

The Wichita Eagle. "Thank Others for Helping Capture Scudder's Slayer." December 1, 1923.

The Wichita Eagle. "Three Surprise Witnesses Tell of 'Wild Party.'" March 9, 1927.

The Wichita Eagle. "3000 Attend Hall Funeral Services." April 16, 1925.

The Wichita Eagle. "Trying to Prove Stallcup's Gun Killed Marshall." November 3, 1927.

The Wichita Eagle. "Two Murder Cases Placed on Docket for April Term." February 22, 1963.

The Wichita Eagle. "Two Trails of Blood Lead Officers to Believe All 3 Wounded by Pal of Victim." August 29, 1927.

The Wichita Eagle. "Underworld 'Tip' Puts Local Police on Slayer's Trail." April 12, 1925.

The Wichita Eagle. "War Declared on Wichita Speeders when Ogden Dies." June 26, 1927.

The Wichita Eagle. "Wichita Man Who Shot it out with Bandit Trio Will Take Survivor to State Pen Today." January 5, 1928.

The Wichita Eagle. "Wichita Mourns Death of Pugh." August 1, 1930.

The Wichita Eagle. "Wichita Police Captain Killed in Gun Battle." May 23, 1915.

The Wichita Eagle. "Wichita Policeman Near Death." November 29, 1923.

The Wichita Eagle. "Wichita Policeman is Slain." November 6, 1921.

The Wichita Eagle. "Widow of Policeman Allowed Pension of Half Husband's Pay." September 3, 1930.

The Wichita Eagle. "Woman Says Slain Man Got Letters Threatening Him." November 8, 1921.

The Wichita Eagle. "Woman Talks of the Slain Man." November 7, 1921.

The Wichita Eagle. "Youth and Convict Nabbed as Slayers of Merle Colver." August 15, 1931.

The Wichita Eagle. "Youth Sought in the Hall Murder is Under Arrest." April 14, 1925.

Wichita Police Department. "Reward: Wanted for Murder." May 22, 1925.

The Wichita Weekly Journal. "Brutal Murder." September 27, 1888.

Williamson, Roger E. *Wichita Police Department: 1871-2000*. Wichita: Wichita Police Benefit Fund Association, 2001.

Windfield Daily Courier. "George Oldham Shot by Foster." December 5, 1921.

Acknowledgements

With this being my first book, I have many people to thank, starting with my family. I was blessed to be raised in a family of public servants who have sacrificed a great deal for the benefit of others. I am a fourth-generation police officer, and a third-generation Wichita police officer. My greatest teacher in life and in the field of policing was my father, retired Lieutenant Philip J. Marceau, who honorably served in the Wichita Police Department for over twenty years. He provided me with invaluable advice throughout my entire life until he died on August 16, 2022. My mother, Susan M. Marceau (Corns), is a former registered nurse who also made a great impact on my life.

My two older brothers, Tony Marceau and Danny Marceau, both were good role models that worked hard in school and while employed. They set good examples for me to follow and helped shape my work ethic. My uncle, Anthony Marceau, retired as Deputy Chief with the Sedgwick County Fire Department. He and my other uncle, Daniel Marceau, a retired Deputy Chief of the Wichita Police Department, both had a great influence on me from a young age.

My biggest supporter has been my wife, Amanda Lynn Marceau (Brummer), who has put up with my terrible work schedule, the many nights of doing homework on my days off, and a long list of holidays missed during the past two decades. Without her willingness to listen and share her thoughts, I do not believe my decisions would have been as wise or my outlook so grand. Her love and support have been absolute and unconditional.

My studies at Wichita State University were a great experience and very beneficial to my career. Many professors were influential, especially in my graduate studies in the History Department. I would like to thank Dr. Robert Owens, Dr. Jay Price, and Dr. George Dehner for sharing their knowledge and expertise.

I appreciate the help of Kevin McKenna, who shared several sources of information that assisted me in writing this book. Chris Ronen's assistance was helpful with the creation of this book's cover. Tony Bamberger's knowledge of the history of the Wichita Police Department helped clear up some questions that I had during the creation of this book. Jordan Jones and Roger Williamson's books on the history of the Wichita Police Department are great contributions to the city and helped me tremendously.

Scott Moon recommended an editor, Kalene Williams. I appreciate both of them, as Kalene made me aware of some bad habits in my writing and recommended necessary changes throughout the book.

ABOUT THE AUTHOR

Christopher P. Marceau is a third-generation Wichita police officer and historian, specializing in American and local history. He was born and raised in Wichita, Kansas, and attended Wichita North High School and Wichita State University, where he received a Bachelor of Business Administration degree in Management and a Master of Arts degree in History. He is married to his wife, Amanda.

Christopher P. Marceau

www.ingramcontent.com/pod-product-compliance
Lightning Source LLC
Chambersburg PA
CBHW061943130526
44582CB00051B/211/J